GORILLA
MARKETING

by

Tony Anderson

**Grosvenor House
Publishing Limited**

This book is published by
Grosvenor House Publishing Ltd
28-30 High Street, Guildford, Surrey, GU1 3HY.
www.grosvenorhousepublishing.co.uk

A CIP record for this book
is available from the British Library

ISBN 978-1-907652-72-1

Dedication

To Daniel, Matthew, Holly and JoJo

Acknowledgements

This book would never have been written if easyJet hadn't got off the ground. So thanks are due, in the first instance, to Nick, Arjun, Anna, Trevor, and all those who were there at the very beginning. It goes without saying that Stelios had the idea, the passion and the money to back it, so I'll use the opportunity to thank him, too.

Thanks are also due to those who helped in the creation of this book: most notably, Tom Tiffin, for his amazing illustrations (www.tombaxtertiffin.com), and David Barrett, for his patient proof-reading.

Finally, the biggest thank-you goes to Kathrin, my wife, for putting up with my monkey obsession for so long!

Front Cover Design: Tom Tiffin
Back Cover Photograph: easyJet

Introduction

Seven a.m. on a cold, damp morning in November 1995. Fifty two tons of steel and aluminium, thirty six miles of wiring and one hundred and thirty five passengers and crew accelerated down the runway at Luton Airport before disappearing into a grey sky. On board the inaugural easyJet flight 11 to Glasgow was Stelios Haji-Ioannou, twenty eight year old multi-millionaire son of a Greek shipping tycoon and the founder of easyJet, Britain's newest and brashest airline. I sat quietly at the back of the plane relieved still to be on board, a number of my colleagues having been unceremoniously off-loaded to make way for a BBC *Panorama* film crew who'd unexpectedly asked if they could join us on the first flight up to Scotland. Stelios was never one to miss a PR opportunity – a fact reflected in the disappointed faces of those left behind in the airport terminal. Perhaps appropriately for the first flight of a no-frills airline the journey was mundane and uneventful. No glitz, glamour or champagne in evidence and the normally ebullient Stelios strangely subdued. Shortly after take-off, he made a brief announcement through the aircraft's PA system, but for once failed to rise to the occasion. On arrival at a damp Glasgow airport we were greeted by the wailing of a lone piper who guided the passengers on their short walk from the aircraft through the drizzling rain to the relative warmth of the terminal building. Stelios and I sat in the incongruous setting of the VIP lounge, thumbing through our coverage in the Scottish morning papers waiting for the aircraft to be cleaned and checked before we boarded for the return trip to London. A group of cabin crew in British Airways uniform smirked as we passed them in the terminal. Our Gorilla bashing adventures had begun!

Getting in shape

"How do you get to be a millionaire? Be a billionaire and start an airline." (Sir Richard Branson)

The business of civil aviation is famously and fabulously unprofitable. A report published by Stanford University in 2000 suggested that the world's airlines suffered cumulative net losses of some $20.4 billion in the five years prior to easyJet's launch. The chill winds of deregulation blowing through the industry forced hundreds of airlines to the wall, taking with them the money of shareholders, investors and taxpayers. Size and illustrious heritage offered no protection. The list of now defunct carriers includes such names as the mighty Pan American Airways, Belgian state airline Sabena and the proud Swissair, all one-time Gorillas of the aviation scene. Mega mergers (like the one between KLM and Air France) and the farce of Chapter 11 bankruptcy protection epitomised the desperate struggle for survival of the European flag carriers and the North American legacy airlines.

If it was tough to survive as a Gorilla, it was even tougher for the new kids on the block. The failure rate among start-up airlines within the first two years of operation ran close to 90%. Hardly surprising, then, that the announcement of easyJet's arrival was greeted with scorn and derision by the industry establishment. "Europe isn't ready for the peanut airline," sneered a British Airways spokesman quoted in the days leading up to our launch.

Yet I was going into this adventure with my eyes open, having first encountered the low-cost airline phenomenon five years earlier while working for BA on a secondment to their New York marketing office. The United States was where it had all began. Deregulation back in the 1970s had spawned a wave of start-ups including Southwest the "Daddy" of low-cost airlines. This triggered not just a price war, but an industry shake-out almost Darwinian in its harshness. Many of the new carriers folded, but amidst the financial carnage Southwest had found a formula that worked. Under the inspired leadership of its legendary Chief Executive, Herb Kelleher, the Dallas-based airline prospered, turning in a tidy profit year after year. Southwest was credited with breaking an effective oligopoly of the big American carriers and changing the face of civil aviation. While living and working in New York, I used my free time to explore North America. As an airline employee, I enjoyed discounted fares with other carriers, but was amazed to find that Southwest's regular prices were often lower than those I could get through British Airways' staff travel programme.

I returned to the UK, convinced the low-cost concept could work in Europe - provided the regulators did their job and ensured fair play. Consequently, in the spring of 1995, when I was approached about taking a job as the Sales and Marketing Director of a new low-cost airline based on the North American model, I was very interested. My interest was heightened further when I learned that the man behind the venture was a young, ambitious Greek entrepreneur with access to considerable financial resources. His name was Stelios Haji-Ioannou.

Having resigned from British Airways four years earlier, I relished the opportunity to cross swords with my former employer. After completing the graduate training programme, I'd joined the marketing distribution side of the business as part of a small team seeking to develop the airline's direct sales. It was a frustrating time. BA had a lot of bright people, but there was an innate conservatism within the company that stifled truly progressive thinking. I'd left with a real feeling of missed opportunity, but here was a once-in-a-lifetime chance to set things straight. Taking on the Gorilla on its home turf would be a formidable challenge. In those days, British Airways was an undisputed 800-pound silverback of the aviation business. Newly privatised, the company was in better financial shape than virtually any other European flag carrier and had demonstrated its ruthlessness with new competitors. To survive and prosper, we'd need to be bold, creative and fast on our feet. This called not just for marketing, but Gorilla marketing.

The first and most important rule to follow when starting an airline (or, indeed, any business) is to have a plan: its importance makes it worth repeating and underlining: "Have a Plan". You can change it, rip it up in frustration and - in future years - look back and laugh at how off the mark it was: but you need to *have a plan*. According to the American General Dwight Eisenhower, no battle plan survives more than five minutes' contact with the enemy, but he still cited the need to "**HAVE A PLAN**". The draft easyJet plan was a thick wad of A4 paper: stamped confidential, it was handed to me with great ceremony on my first day as an easyJet employee. Having been told to guard the document with my life, I promptly left it on a tube train somewhere between Green Park and King's Cross. I bluffed my way through meetings and sweated it out for the few days it took me to get hold of another copy.

The easyJet business plan was largely a financial and operational plan to which I was to provide marketing input. Finance Director, Nick Manoudakis (with the help of industry consultant, Peter Leishman) had done much of the legwork, with Stelios providing the strategic direction. The plan was well structured, meticulous in its detail yet significantly different from the airline's eventual business model. It contained no mention of 100% direct sales or internet distribution, both cornerstones of easyJet's long-term success. The section on pricing stated that £29 was to be our absolutely lowest fare on any route: below that level, we lost money. At that point, had someone told me that within a decade low-cost carriers would not only be flying tens of millions of passengers for fares as low as 99p but would also be among the most profitable airlines in history, I would have dismissed them as a raving lunatic. With the benefit of hindsight, it's not hard to find fault with the original plan. Yet, for all its flaws, it provided a structure and a general sense of direction, allowing the management team to stay focussed in those early months when it would have been all too easy to succumb to distractions.

Financial discipline was firmly enshrined in the business plan, and rightly so: many start-up airlines fail because they simply run out of cash to pay the bills. Life as an airline is all about managing cash, because the bills for fuel, air-traffic control and airport charges (not to mention wages) are unceasing - even in the depths of winter, when passengers are less inclined to fly. Ever wary of the possibility of airlines going bust; airports, fuel companies and other key suppliers are unforgiving in their management of debtors. If the new venture was to have a fighting chance, it would need cash - and lots of it. Fortunately, the young man behind the venture had money: an initial five million pounds borrowed from his father to start the airline, and access to more if he needed it. But easyJet was to be no rich kid's plaything. Stelios was determined that the airline would have a ruthless approach to cost management. From day one, no-frills was to mean exactly that.

We started the airline with two leased Boeing 737s, the workhorse for budget airlines over the years. Ours were the 737-200 version, each seating 130 passengers. By the standards of today's gleaming low-cost fleets, they were slightly long in the tooth: if you looked closely, you could see that the carpets were fraying. But they were safe, relatively efficient jets and passengers seemed happy enough. Pilots and senior cabin crew were contracted in, as was most of the training and our airport ground-handling services. At this stage, we didn't have our own air operating certificate, so we worked under the certificate of Air Foyle, a Luton-based air-transportation company. We were described by some as a virtual airline, but it was the fastest and most cost-effective way for us to get off the ground.

The original business plan assumed easyJet would operate out of Stansted, a natural choice at the time - or so thought Nick (he'd found a house within easy commuting distance of the Essex airport!). We'd only entered into negotiations with Luton as a means of securing a better deal from Stansted. On a hastily arranged visit to Luton with Operations Director Dave McCulloch, Stelios liked what he saw. The airport was clearly underutilised, and its biggest customers were large charter operators like Thomson and Monarch to whom we subcontracted our engineering. The airport's management was desperate to secure more scheduled services and willing to cut a deal. As easyJet's Marketing Director and the man responsible for selling the virtues of our new home to potential customers, I winced when Stelios announced that he was going for Luton. In the minds of millions, the airport was associated with flip-flops, straw donkeys and actress Lorraine Chase (star of an infamous advertising campaign for Campari back in the 80s). To gain a better understanding of the airport's history, Stelios and I met Lorraine for tea at the stuffy Hurlingham polo club in London. There was a minor altercation at the door when they insisted we put on ties before being let in. The price of admission was to lose a bet with a colleague that I could avoid wearing a tie in my new job.

We weren't setting out to be a niche airline. Our target market was defined as people who paid the fares out of their own pocket. That meant pretty much everyone except for corporate travellers. The launch marketing budget suggested in the plan was £64,000. I initially thought this was a joke, then saw it as a challenge. Large-scale campaigns of the kind I'd envisaged when I joined were out of the question. What's more, on that kind of money full-service advertising agencies were also ruled out. To make the numbers work, we'd rely heavily on self-generated PR and home-made, low-cost ads in the classified sections of newspapers.

If I were to be so bold as to offer a second piece of advice to anyone launching a new business, it would be probably be: *start as you mean to go on*. Stelios came from a background of wealth and luxury, but instilled a culture of cost consciousness in his new airline from day one. Salaries were modest (even by industry standards), hours were long and office accommodation was basic.

I'd spent my first six weeks working for Stelios, based on the first floor of a swanky townhouse on Curzon Street in the heart of Mayfair. We shared the building with the UK-based staff of our Greek owner's shipping company, Stelmar. Clearly, this was no place to start a low-cost airline: any illusions I might have had about the quality of our working environment were shattered on my first trip to our new home at Luton airport. The contrast was dramatic - a large, shabby open-plan office with paint peeling from the walls inside a large tin shack. This was to be home for the half a dozen people who made up easyJet back in July 1995.

We assembled six grey functional steel desks purchased from an office supply shop, wondering where to put them. When it comes to seating, there's an unwritten convention that the boss takes first pick. Prime position in our case would have been next to the window, looking out on the airport taxiway. Stelios, however, was quick to announce that he would place his desk outside the gents' toilet, the worst possible desk location in the room. The precedent having been set, the rest of us felt no inclination to argue about where we would sit.

For the next twelve years, easyJet was to occupy the same modest offices in Luton, an extraordinary achievement given the airline's spectacular growth over that period. Christened "easyLand", with roof and walls painted in bright orange (what else?), the offices were the first thing most passengers saw when their flights touched down on the Luton tarmac. One employee remarked that the only two man-made constructions visible from space were the Great Wall of China and the easyJet offices at Luton airport. As the airline expanded, the temptation to move to more spacious and less utilitarian accommodation was resisted. The demand for extra space was initially met by demolishing the adjacent spectator's area, much to the chagrin of Luton's plane-spotting community, and then by stacking portakabins on top of one another in the car park outside.

It is a little known fact that the start-up airline was originally going to be named Stelair. This was a logical enough extension, given that our founder had already set up a shipping company called Stelmar. However, shortly before I joined, Stelios had a change of heart. I've heard various accounts of how the name easyJet was decided upon, but according to the version I recall the name was settled on in the unglamorous setting of the back of a Glasgow taxi. Stelios and Finance Director, Nick Manoudakis, batted ideas back and forth before Stelios settled on the name easyJet. The choice of orange as our corporate colour was also down to the airline's Greek Cypriot founder who told me he wanted a colour he could "own" and that wasn't associated with any other European airline. Stelios went for the brightest, boldest most shocking shade of orange we could find: Pantone 021c, or "easyJet orange" as some called it. Sitting in front of a Mac in a small print-design company on a run-down Luton industrial estate, we worked late into the night, refining the logo and typeface ("Cooper Black", if you really want to know!), that have evolved over the years into a hugely successful brand identity.

For any new airline, there are effectively two launch dates. The most obvious is the day of the first flight, but the more commercially significant is the day your seats go on sale. With the clock ticking down to the launch date, we chose a reservations system and set up a small call centre in a corner of our Luton offices. Through the local job centre, we advertised for twenty staff to man the phones. They were to be paid on commission, with no cap on earnings; most were young and had little or no previous experience, all were highly enthusiastic. With the internet and broadband yet to take off, telephone calls were our lifeblood. The centre was to be staffed twenty-four hours a day, seven days a week. "I've lost the key," Stelios was fond of saying.

Some weeks later, we found the right man to run the call centre. John Macleod was an unflappable north Londoner and fanatical Arsenal supporter, tough as nails but with a heart of gold. He'd previously managed a telephone betting operation for Ladbrokes. With easyJet operating a strict no-refunds policy, we figured his experience of telling punters they couldn't have their money back would come in handy.

As October approached, the pace quickened and successive pre-launch actions were ticked off. We appointed a Chief Pilot, Chief Engineer and Head of Cabin Crew. The one-room office at easyLand was starting to get crowded. On the marketing front, I'd got over the size of the launch budget: things were looking up! I recruited an assistant to help with PR, and Nick was persuaded to release more money for our launch. The budget increase brought radio advertising within reach and, with the help of talented industry freelancers, Murray Partridge and Simon Confino, we recorded a couple of crude but effective radio spots. Most of the remaining marketing budget was deployed across local press in Luton, London and Scotland. We'd placed a few modest ads in the classified sections of the national papers but somehow I doubted the BA Gorilla was quaking in his boots. It was October 1995. After months of frenetic activity everything was finally in place - easyJet was cleared for take-off.

The launch

"Europe isn't ready for the peanut airline" (British Airways spokesman quoted in *The Times*)

Six weeks prior to the inaugural flight, easyJet was launched in a blaze of publicity at Planet Hollywood in London's West End. The choice of a (then) fashionable fast-food eatery as our launch venue marked a clear departure from convention. Our judgement was that few journalists would make the trip to Luton even for the novelty value of a plucky upstart airline, so we'd make it as easy as possible for them by staging the launch in central London, throwing in free food and drink to improve turnout.

Much of what we were to announce was already in the public domain; easyJet would be based at Luton, operating initially to Scotland, and our aircraft would be Boeing 737s. The big secret, closely guarded from the media and the reason why many of the journalists were turning up, was the exact level of our fares. It therefore came as something of a shock to hear one of our newly recorded ads blaring out the price on Capital Radio as I drove down to London en route to the launch. Fortunately for me, the boss wasn't listening to Capital that morning and the errant ad proved to have been an isolated slip that failed to find its way into the morning's news bulletins.

On stage in the screening room at Planet Hollywood, Stelios gave an assured performance to the assembled crowd of business and travel journalists. He proudly announced that easyJet's first routes from Luton to Glasgow and Edinburgh would be priced from £29 one way, or - as Stelios put it - "flying for the price of a pair of jeans". There followed a series of one-to-ones with individual journalists, clearly relishing the opportunity to get up close and personal with someone as articulate, outspoken and provocative as the airline's young founder. Two hours later, and with mission accomplished, we piled into a taxi for the journey back to Luton. By the time we got back to the office, the telephones in our understaffed call centre were ringing off the hooks. Beaming from ear to ear, the proud owner of a newly launched airline took a seat in the call centre, put on a headset and started taking bookings from customers. In all my years working for Stelios, I don't think I ever saw him happier than at that moment.

Thumbing through the following day's press reports of the launch, I was astounded by the extent of the coverage we had achieved. Almost every national newspaper had covered our launch; little matter that collectively they had little faith in our long-term survival. What counted was that all of them had mentioned the price. Of course, by today's standards a £29 fare is nothing special, but back in 1995 it was sensational news - particularly when viewed against the backdrop of British Airways' cheapest one-way fare, priced at £120. These were halcyon days in another respect: back then, there were no air passenger duties, no credit-card fees, baggage charges or priority boarding to guarantee a seat with the rest of your family. The price quoted by the telephone salesperson for your flight was the price you paid. End of story.

Despite the fact that the birth of easyJet made for good copy, we might never have made the impact we did. But we got lucky - the story had broken on an exceptionally quiet news day. "Air wars over London" screamed the headline in the London Evening Standard. We'd made the front pages. The public's reaction? Well, to put it simply: people saw the price and picked up the phone.

With hindsight, the pivotal decision we took in putting together the easyJet business model was to sell our flights 100% direct to our customers. At that time, airlines typically sold only a small proportion of their seats direct to the public, mainly over the telephone and through airport ticket offices. The majority were sold through travel agents who had a strong grip on the distribution chain. Ours was to be the first airline anywhere in the world to completely cut out the middleman. This was a bold decision, putting clear blue water between easyJet and every other airline on the planet. But it wasn't a total shot in the dark: key trends were working in our favour. Not only did the UK have the world's second highest penetration of credit cards, but there was an established culture of buying over the telephone, with the likes of First Direct Bank and Direct Line having blazed a trail for us to follow.

From a marketing standpoint, selling direct allowed easyJet to position itself as the airline that cut out the middleman, a concept that consumers were increasingly equating with lower prices. While travel agents weren't reviled by the great British public, they weren't exactly loved either. Consequently, they became an early target for our tongue-in-cheek advertising campaigns. "Cut out the middleman, fly to Scotland for just £29" proclaimed our adverts in bold type above a cartoon image of a travel agent in a cheap suit with a cheesy grin. "Its brown trouser time for travel agents" went one of our radio tag-lines. A stronger ad featured Stelios putting a stake through the heart of a Dracula-style cartoon travel agent with the strapline "At easyJet we know how to deal with bloodsuckers". At the last minute, I bottled out from running this one - not least because I'd spent the three years of my life prior to easyJet working for Thomas Cook, one of the UK's best-known travel agents. The travel agency community was livid; already faced with reductions in commission payments from the larger airlines, the insults from this insolent upstart must have been difficult to bear. Before the launch, a spokesman from the powerful Scottish Passenger Agents Association was quoted as saying that we'd never sell a flight in Scotland without them. Several million flights later, they were left looking pretty stupid.

Our stance on commission meant easyJet's relationship with travel agents was always going to be problematic, but no one could accuse us of failing to be up-front about where we stood. Stelios set the tone at an industry conference where he was asked to present to a group of senior travel agency executives. In front of a packed hall and with bodyguard in tow, he announced to a disbelieving audience "the relationship between us is simple: I hate you and you hate me".

The following year, a double booking meant he was unable to make a scheduled repeat appearance in front of an audience of nearly two thousand at the Association of British Travel Agents convention in Tenerife. Instead, at short notice, he asked me to speak in his place. I was nervous: there were no heavies to back me up in the event of trouble, and I confess to having thoroughly investigated the exit routes for the conference hall prior to taking the stand. My presentation was entitled "Why easyJet will never pay commission to travel agents". I elected to skip over a slide depicting a large orange asteroid headed towards a group of cartoon dinosaurs. Throughout my speech the audience in the vast conference hall remained largely silent and surly. I fielded a couple of rambling questions and sat down, concerned at what might come next. I needn't have been worried. To my amazement, the ire of the audience was directed not at myself, but at the British Airways Commercial Director, Dan Brewin, who chose this opportunity to announce that the airline would be cutting the commission they paid to travel agents. "At least easyJet are being honest with us," a travel agent confided to me over a drink in the hotel bar. "BA don't seem to realise that they can't survive without us". Fourteen years on, with high-street travel agents playing an increasingly marginalised role in a restructured industry, his words have a hollow ring to them.

The more the travel agents protested, the more we persisted in goading them. Large Ghostbusters-style posters appeared around the area declaring the airport to be a "travel-agent-free zone". Luton's Marketing Director complained to me that "anti travel agent" stickers had been found stuck to the walls of the airport toilets and were proving difficult to remove. I denied responsibility and made a mental note to order some more.

Some months later, in a further escalation of hostilities, we ran a competition among our passengers to design an easyJet sick bag. The prize - a couple of free flights - was hardly a jackpot win, but we got a sackful of entries. The winner submitted a suitably derogatory picture with the caption "Sick of paying for travel agents?" The campaign was great fun, but we were making a serious point in a light-hearted way. There was simply not enough fat in the price of easyJet's flights for a middleman to take a cut.

With the airline having committed itself to the direct sales route, the choice of telephone number became a topic of heated discussion among the management team. Memorable telephone numbers were expensive but vital for a direct sales business in pre-internet times. We finally settled on the Luton number 01582 445566. Purchased from a local taxi company by our hard-nosed negotiator, Arjun Batra, and painted in lurid orange on the aircraft fuselage, it certainly made an impact. Having initially congratulated myself for coming up with the idea of plastering the telephone number on our planes, I was slightly concerned how the idea might be adapted when, one year later, we began services to Amsterdam. The short-term solution was simple: put the Dutch number on one side and the English number on the other side of the aircraft. However, as we planned our international expansion, the penny dropped that the concept simply wasn't scalable. Thankfully, the universality of the internet came to the rescue and the telephone numbers were eventually replaced with what has become the trademark easyJet.com.

We didn't actually paint our aircraft with the telephone numbers or indeed any of the promotional message or designs employed in the early years. Instead we relied on special decals which had the advantage of being quick to apply and remove. This makes eminent sense given that the biggest cost of painting a leased plane is not the labour or materials, but the leasing costs which still have to be paid when the aircraft is sitting on the ground for two days waiting for the paint to dry. Delivering marketing messages through the creative use of decals proved to be an effective tool, well suited to easyJet's highly tactical marketing approach. Not all our marketing ideas worked however. We somehow contrived to name one of our planes after the Scottish band "Big Country" just as the group's popularity started to wane. A couple of months after naming the aircraft, the decals were quietly removed and telephone calls requesting an explanation from the band's manager went unanswered.

The razzmatazz of easyJet's launch barely caused a ripple in the boardrooms of the Gorillas of European aviation. We'd managed to get off the ground (which is more than can be said for many start-up airlines), but the idea that we posed any kind of threat to the big boys seemed laughable. We now stood at a crossroads: would we take on the British Airways 800 pound Gorilla in a no-holds barred fight, or would we adopt a less confrontational strategy, staying under their radar? For easyJet, there was only ever going to be one way forward, but the option of growing quietly and avoiding direct confrontation with a Gorilla was a path chosen by others with more modest aspirations.

Small niche carriers had been a feature of the airline landscape for decades. Typically, these baby airlines ran operations from secondary airports, used small aircraft, charged relatively high fares and - importantly - posed no significant threat to the big guys. One such airline was Suckling Airways, a small Luton-based outfit run by husband and wife team, Roy and Merlyn Suckling. When easyJet first came to Luton, Suckling Airways was operating flights to Amsterdam and Paris. They had a small and (what they believed to be) loyal customer base, drawn mainly from the local catchment area. Their passengers were willing to pay a premium for the convenience of Luton, rather than travel round the M25 to Heathrow or Gatwick. There were just about enough of these customers to fill a propeller driven Dornier aircraft that shuttled back and forth to the continent two or three times daily. The aeroplane was noisy and cramped, seating around twenty-four passengers at full capacity. At Stelios' insistence, I took a trip from Paris to Luton on Suckling Airways, an experience I can only describe as being like riding bareback on a giant bumble bee. It was hardly surprising, therefore, that when easyJet commenced flights to Amsterdam in April 1996, their passengers began deserting in droves. I must confess to feeling a twinge of guilt - and even sadness - when I learned that Suckling was to stop flying from Luton airport. Oh, and if you're ever contemplating a flight on one of the smaller Dornier aircraft, bear in mind that some of them don't have toilets. Otherwise, you could end up sitting cross-legged for the whole flight - like the author of this book!

The autumn of 1995 turned into winter, traditionally the season where passenger demand is lowest and financially weak airlines come under pressure. But, with a big brash launch under our belt, the call centre running smoothly and our two aircraft shuttling between Luton and Scotland, I felt proud of what we had achieved and quietly confident about our future. The months of planning and hard work had paid off. Admittedly, our success in getting off the ground owed more than a little to Lady Luck, but we were hardly complaining. With what lay ahead, easyJet would need all the luck it could get.

Ape about advertising

"Don't tell my mother I work in advertising, she thinks I play piano in a whorehouse."
(Jacques Seguera)

The new orange airline was born on a wave of newspaper headlines and PR stunts. Yet while the deliberate courting of controversy can generate significant awareness and is undoubtedly cost-effective, on its own it's not enough to build a brand. It took a multi-million-pound investment in above-the-line advertising to sustain easyJet and support our PR campaign at a critical stage in the airline's development. Our arch rival, British Airways, had a huge advertising budget and was able to target specific routes tactically through their "world offers" programme. From the moment we launched, I knew it would only be a matter of time before the Gorilla turned its considerable marketing firepower on us.

For any Marketing Director, but particularly the Marketing Director of a start-up airline, determining where to spend your finite advertising budget is a vexing question. In the early days of easyJet, press advertising was our medium of choice. This was the mid 90s, and the internet was still in its infancy: the low-cost, targeted search advertising favoured by modern start-ups simply wasn't an option open to us. The decision to focus on press rather than broadcast advertising was not just about cost, but also had something to do with the constraints of having to secure pre-broadcast approval from the radio and TV clearance authorities. This tended to blunt the spontaneity and topicality that we always sought to engender in our advertising. For easyJet, speed was always of the essence: whatever appeared in the previous day's news columns was viewed as a potential hook for the next day's advertising. We learned from experience that the newspapers rarely complained about our ads, however provocative they might be. What's more, the Advertising Standards Authority who regulated press advertising appeared to have blunt teeth. By contrast, the broadcast authorities could simply refuse to approve any advertising if they felt it failed to meet their strict criteria. And without their approval, the ad wouldn't run! Stelios was generally very good at controlling his temper, but watching him argue over the telephone with a faceless bureaucrat over the semantics of a particular script was like witnessing an irresistible force meet an immoveable object. On the occasions that the immoveable object triumphed, I learned to keep out of the Boss's way for a few hours afterwards.

The airline's strong visual identity and simple price offer made outdoor advertising via posters and billboards a particularly effective means of getting its message across. I found a local sign writer who'd got hold of a batch of particularly lurid orange paint: not quite our official shade, but near enough. We leased a number of large billboards in key sites around Luton, including one in the car park directly opposite the railway station. The billboards were hand-painted and depicted a cartoon aeroplane together with the message "Scotland from £29". Within a matter of days, I started receiving complaints that the "shocking orange" made the posters too visible. Some claimed that we were distracting drivers. One angry resident even suggested that we were impacting local property prices. Something was clearly working.

In our negotiations with Luton over landing fees, we'd persuaded the authorities to give us a significant number of prime poster sites around the airport. At the last minute, we insisted they throw in advertising on the luggage trolleys too. All were adorned with the same crude (but effective) orange messaging. We offered to repaint the scruffy waiting room at Luton railway station in return for having an easyJet poster in the station concourse. The offer was accepted, but the contractor got a little carried away and painted one of the walls orange instead of white. To Luton's inhabitants, it must have seemed as if the whole town were turning orange. Like a dog marking its territory, we wanted everyone passing through the area to know that easyJet had arrived and that this was our patch.

Although we had consciously elected not to use a full-service advertising agency, we did need to work with a media-buying company. Matters Media was a small but fast-growing independent agency based in central London. It was owned by Mike Hellens, an easy-going and personable character, whose wife, Abigail, worked for MTV and had known Stelios when he first arrived in London as a student. Mike may have been laid-back, but he was a shrewd businessman. Matters Media's growth was due mainly to his having landed Carphone Warehouse as a client when the mobile retailer was in start-up mode a few years earlier. Throughout easyJet's early years, Mike and his team were at the sharp end, coping admirably with a stream of short-notice requests for keenly priced advertising space to support our highly tactical campaigns.

"Half the money I spend on advertising is wasted; the trouble is I don't know which half." is a famous quote attributed to John Wanamaker a US department-store magnate in the 1920s. The fact that virtually all easyJet's early advertising was direct response gave us a big advantage in determining what was working. Initially, we used a single telephone number in all our ads and, as part of the booking process, our call-centre staff were required to ask customers where they'd heard about easyJet, selecting the appropriate response from a drop-down list. The flaws in this approach were highlighted when the figures told us that the newspaper that had generated more calls than all the others put together was the *Aberdeen Press and Journal.* The Scottish title just happened to appear first in the alphabetically sorted drop-down list from which staff selected the responses. Lesson learnt, we adopted a new approach that involved using a different telephone number in each of our press advertising campaigns. This time, we were able to attribute the calls that came in on a particular number to the relevant paper. This proved a crude but reliable means of measuring advertising effectiveness. It also helped us focus our advertising spend in those papers where we believed we would get the most bang for our buck. Such an approach sounds laughably rudimentary in an age when marketeers take for granted the high levels of accountability associated with internet advertising. But, back then, our approach was breaking new ground and giving us a clear edge over our competitors who, for the most part, were selling through travel agents and, consequently, had a much poorer handle on the cost-effectiveness of their marketing campaigns.

I spoke regularly to our call-centre staff to better understand how customers were learning about easyJet. One of our agents informed me that, when asked how he'd got hold of our telephone number, a locally based customer had responded as follows. "I'd heard about easyJet on the radio but never knew much about it. Then, one day, I was mowing my lawn when one of your planes flew low over my garden...seeing the number written on the side of the plane, I rushed into the house, grabbed a pen and wrote it down!"

In our first couple of years at Luton, we worked with a small, local design and print company called White Knight, located on a grim industrial estate a few miles from the airport. I'd found them in the local edition of Yellow Pages while searching for someone to help us with the creation and production of our press ads. The very antithesis of a West-End advertising agency, the staff at White Knight were unpretentious, flexible and willing to work hard on a limited budget. Throughout 1995 and 1996, I spent many hours with Stelios at White Knight's offices, huddled round a Macintosh computer having great fun designing ads off the cuff. It was in one of the early sessions with White Knight's chief designer, Barry Debenham, that the idea of painting the telephone number on the side of the aeroplane and the original version of the easyJet cartoon plane were born.

The young airline's visual identity was constantly evolving over the first years of its existence. Cartoon representations of the easyJet aircraft gradually gave way to line drawings and photographs as it became apparent that many of our customers were unaware of one of our biggest strengths: the relatively young age of our aeroplanes. Indeed, at a rare research focus group session a number of the participants revealed they thought we operated old propeller-driven aircraft. Stelios was quick to pick up on the marketing potential of having a young fleet. Not long after we'd got rid of our older leased aircraft and replaced them with shiny new Boeings, this was developed into a key advertising theme. I was constantly struck by the reaction of first-time easyJet fliers, pleasantly surprised by the shiny new aeroplanes on which they were travelling. Exceeding limited customer expectations is what being a successful low-cost airline is about.

With a rise in the frequency of services on our Anglo-Scottish routes, filling our planes meant growing the market, not just grabbing share from existing operators. Implicitly, this meant attracting passengers who would normally use the railways. We singled out infrastructure operator Railtrack and the train operators for some serious Gorilla treatment. They proved a good target. The newly privatised railway companies were unloved and regarded with considerable suspicion by the general public.

Back in 1995, the rail franchise for the East Coast main line between London and Scotland was operated by an outfit who called themselves GNER. It sounded less like the name of a train company, more like the noise you make when a cricket ball hits you between the legs. We drew up plans for an aggressive poster-based campaign that would highlight the price differences between plane and train. I anticipated there might be a request to tone down the advertising copy, but when we tried to secure prime sites at London's Kings Cross and Edinburgh Waverley stations, there was a mysterious lack of availability. It looked like someone had been tipped off.

Undeterred, we decided on a different angle of attack. Tapping into a topical, high-profile news story, we took out full-page ads in the *London*

Evening Standard and the Scottish press depicting a cartoon snail looking aghast at a large leaf on the line under the heading "Snailtrack". Humour must have been a commodity in short supply in the rail industry, for we received polite requests (which, needless to say, we ignored) to withdraw these ads that "were causing considerable offence". This was but one of a number of instances where requests for the withdrawal of advertisements led to the extension of the life of an ad campaign. The "snail ad" was framed and fixed to the wall behind Stelios' desk in easyLand, with the picture of the cartoon travel agent alongside. A pattern was starting to emerge.

The film "Brewster's Millions" was a minor hit in the late 80s. The main character is a down-and-out baseball player who has to spend $30 million in thirty days in order to inherit his true fortune of $300 million. Not only was it a great movie, it was also cult viewing among the easyJet management team. Starting an airline is undoubtedly a great way to dissipate a Brewster-sized fortune, but one of the few alternative ways of burning cash at a comparable rate is to become involved with football. We wisely rebutted approaches to become involved in the sponsorship of teams, including struggling local side Luton Town, and instead looked to the "beautiful game" as an area of opportunity. A steep rise in the number of European club matches and the success of British clubs on the European stage was generating significant demand for cheap flights, particularly in the winter months when holiday traffic fell away. Before easyJet's revenue-management system became fully automated, I recall sitting with our call-centre manager listening to *Radio 5's* live broadcast of the Champions League draw. His finger would be poised, ready to adjust prices depending on who was playing who. We learnt from experience that football fans moved quickly to secure their travel arrangements, and we weren't the only ones with our fingers poised over buttons. Unless we reacted and adjusted our prices immediately, flights could sell out in a matter of minutes - sometimes, in seconds. It was tempting to rack prices up as high as they would go, but we were careful not to overdo it. Sometimes, the better solution was to put on extra capacity rather than alienate passengers by raising fares to levels that the likes of British Airways were charging.

In their battle to get the best possible prices, budget-conscious soccer fans were working out creative new ways to beat the system. As the low-cost airlines expanded at an accelerating pace, many more points on the European map became linked to a vast, inter-connecting low-cost network. At its simplest, being a successful low-cost airline means moving large numbers of people from point A to point B and, of course, varying fares appropriately, depending on the level of demand at any given point in time. However, the proliferation of low-cost routes meant that, in certain circumstances, flying from point A to point B via point C might actually be cheaper than flying from A to B direct.

The *Telegraph's* website cited the case of a journey from Bournemouth to Glasgow where the quickest way to reach the Scottish city was not by car or train, but to travel on Ryanair via Barcelona. The twist in this particular tale was that diverting to the continent was not only faster, but cheaper too. Football fans were quick to work out these alternative routings, causing problems not only for airline revenue managers, but for their equivalents in the rail industry too. The same *Telegraph* story reported how a Liverpool football fan from north London flew from London to Liverpool via Brussels to watch his team play against Aston Villa. Amazingly, the flights ended up costing him less than half the price of a return train ticket. Andy Rolle and his friend, Chris, apparently paid £100 for two return flights. This compared with the £204 Virgin Trains wanted for two return tickets to Merseyside. The two men arrived at Stansted airport in Essex at 6.45 a.m. for a 7.30 a.m. flight, landed in Brussels an hour later and took a flight to Liverpool an hour after that, arriving at 11.45 a.m. "It was perfect," Mr Rolle said, "especially when we beat Villa 1-0. But it's the first time I've needed my passport to see Liverpool play at Anfield."

In the fifteen years since easyJet first burst onto the scene, the advertising battleground has shifted away from traditional media towards the brave new world of digital marketing. It's no understatement to say that the arrival of the internet changed airline advertising for ever. In common with other carriers, easyJet today spends a large proportion of its now multi-million-pound marketing budget online. Search-based advertising and a proliferation of intermediary sites allow the smallest of start-ups with the most modest of budgets to make their offering available to prospective customers world-wide. Through judicious selection of search terms, money can be targeted at a specific route or a particular competitor. The tiniest regional airline is able to compete with the biggest, hairiest Gorilla. Every click a customer makes and every penny the advertiser spends can be measured and reported on a real-time basis. The principle of accountable airline advertising pioneered by easyJet has truly come of age.

Breaking the mould

"Stupidity is doing the same thing and expecting different results." (Anon)

Anyone passing through Luton airport towards the end of 1995 had only to glance at the runway to see that easyJet was visibly and undeniably different. But it wasn't just the bright orange lettering on its planes and the lurid uniforms of the cabin crew that caused the young upstart to stand out from its peers. We'd intentionally set out to create a fundamentally different kind of airline, a company where questioning the established way of doing things was the norm.

Being the world's first carrier to go one hundred percent direct saved us a small fortune in travel-agents' commission and computer-reservations fees. This crucial decision also allowed easyJet to operate as a ticketless airline from day one, generating further savings on printing, postage and accounting for tickets. To make things simple, we took a firm line with customers whose arrangements changed. Once a flight was booked, cancellations and refunds were not permitted. Our policy was strictly "use it or lose it".

Compared with conventional airlines, our aircraft were highly utilised, flying from early in the morning until late at night. Speedy twenty-minute turnarounds (the time the plane spends on the tarmac between flights) and the simplicity of our operating model allowed easyJet to "sweat" its most expensive assets. Traditional airline boarding cards were replaced with bright orange, re-usable laminated boarding tags numbered 1 to 130. Not only did this save on paper, it also encouraged passengers to show up early for check-in since they were boarded in numerical order, starting with the lowest.

Starting with a blank sheet of paper, we looked for savings everywhere. The only exception was safety, which could never be compromised. Stelios had experienced the trauma of a major accident some years previously when an oil tanker called *The Haven* leased by his father's shipping company *Troodos* had blown-up with loss of life, causing a major pollution incident off the Italian coastline. There followed a legal battle in the Italian courts that dragged on for many years, with Stelios and his father facing manslaughter charges before being fully and finally acquitted on all counts in 2002. Unsurprisingly, the commitment of easyJet's owner to running a safe operation was absolute: "If you think safety's expensive, try having an accident," he would tell us. As if it were needed, a stark reminder of the safety imperative came in May 1996 when ValuJet flight 592, en route from Miami to Atlanta, crashed into a Florida swamp killing all 110 passengers and crew on board.

Safety aside, pretty much everything else was fair game when it came to cost cutting. The complimentary onboard meals that were *de rigueur* back in those days were an early casualty. Quite what had persuaded European airlines that passengers needed to be given something to eat on flights of such short duration, I will never know. British Airways prided itself on the hot breakfasts available on its early-morning flights from London to Scotland. The cost of providing such a service in the air was a multiple of what it cost on the ground. We had no intention of participating in such madness. Stelios was fond of saying "there's no such thing as a free lunch", and so it proved as easyJet introduced its onboard easyKiosk, selling snacks that competitors were giving away for free. When British Airway's catering staff went on strike, easyJet produced an opportunistic ad promising that its own catering staff would never strike as they didn't have any!

Our quest to find ways of doing things differently also proved to be a lot of fun, as the selection process for the first easyJet crew uniform showed. It was decided early on that we didn't want to do anything with the uniforms of the cockpit crew. Unsurprisingly, perhaps, passengers expect their pilots to look like pilots, and authority is generally reinforced through the wearing of a uniform. For the cabin crew, however, we wanted to stand out from the crowd - and here was an opportunity to be quite radical. A number of US carriers, including Southwest Airlines, had already demonstrated that casual cabin crew uniforms were welcomed by passengers and crew alike, although the baggy shorts favoured in the Texas climate would probably be less acceptable to someone disembarking passengers on a cold February morning in Inverness.

We started out with very few preconceptions other than a desire to keep the uniform costs as low as possible. We'd had expressions of interest from a number of suppliers who liked the idea of kitting out an airline. In the summer of 1995, they came to easyLand to present their ideas and their prices - and went away empty-handed. In traditional easyJet style, we thought we could do better ourselves. Not only that: buying something "off the shelf" would mean significantly lower cost. Stelios and I made a trip in my battered Ford Mondeo to the *Next* store in Harpenden, a few miles from Luton. We then loaded up with a selection of jackets, shirts and trousers before taking the clothes back to easyLand, where staff took part in an impromptu modelling session. The verdict was a big thumbs down. The outfits may have been casual, but they were insufficiently distinctive and failed to capture the imagination. We'd also learned that there were Civil Aviation Authority rules in place covering the use of certain synthetic fabrics for crew uniforms.

Then Anna, our ultra-efficient Office Manager at easyLand, mentioned that she'd seen someone wandering around wearing a fantastic orange polo shirt with a Benetton logo. I was duly dispatched to the nearest Benetton shop in Milton Keynes where, indeed, there was a polo shirt and a matching sweatshirt, both in garish easyJet orange, matching the "official" colour almost perfectly. Excited by my discovery, I called Stelios who was so enthused he instructed me to come back to easyLand, pick him up and drive him to Milton Keynes. When he saw the shirts, Stelios was suitably impressed: he pulled out his credit card and duly bought all the orange polos and sweatshirts in the shop (this amounted to around eight of each, in a variety of different sizes). Feedback from the team back at easyLand was positive. What's more, this time the fabrics met with Civil Aviation Authority requirements. I immediately set about trying to place an order for a couple of hundred shirts from Benetton in Italy. This proved more difficult than it sounds since Benetton do not keep central stock, particularly of gaudy colours that go out of fashion as quickly as they come in. Undeterred, I undertook a road trip around London visiting a number of Benetton stores, including outlets in Islington, Brent Cross and Oxford Street. It's hard to imagine quite what the sales staff made of this strange character who came in off the streets, took all the orange sweatshirts and polo shirts off the shelves and stuffed them into a large bag. By the end of my UK shopping tour, I had accumulated around one hundred and fifty shirts of various sizes, piled high in a storage room at easyLand. I joked to Stelios that in our recruitment drive (which we were shortly to begin) we'd need to find twelve "Large", twenty "Medium" and eighty "Small" cabin crew to fit the uniforms we'd bought.

I was determined that the marketing department would run in a very different fashion to that at British Airways. By mid 1996, the weekly marketing meeting held at easyLand provided a focal point for the airline's commercial activities, becoming a key decision-making forum. The easyJet commercial team was young, bright, close-knit and featured future stars of the travel business like Steve Burns, Liz Savage and Gio Picciano. Meetings were structured and business-like, but they were enjoyable too - often punctuated with humour. Stelios would sometimes attend. In fact, it was he who introduced the dubious innovation of holding the meetings standing up "to keep them short". Truth be told, the meetings ran on twice as long when the airline's founder was in attendance. After two or three hours, participants would be leaning on chairs, walls or whatever came to hand If Stelios left the meeting for any reason, we all immediately sat down. I kept a battery-powered soft-toy Gorilla hidden in the drawer of my desk which bore more than a passing resemblance to our Chairman. When switched on, it would shuffle around making squawking noises and waving its arms in an animated fashion. Bringing out the gorilla was a great way to lighten the mood when Stelios was out of town.

Throwing large parties, bringing the airline's staff together to celebrate and let off steam was hardly an easyJet invention. Virgin, Southwest and, to be fair, a number of conventional airlines had a reputation for partying hard. But it was hardly surprising, given the young age of our staff, that mass parties rapidly became a highlight of the easyJet social calendar. The first such party was staged on the eve of our launch in *Blues West Fourteen*, a basement blues club in West Kensington. It was a high-spirited affair, but involved fewer than a hundred people, most of whom successfully made it into work the following morning to answer phone calls from our first customers. Those early days also saw memorable parties at Stelios' homes in London and Monaco, but these were strictly one-offs.

As easyJet grew, the staff parties became larger, with a lot of creative thinking and planning involved. The space-themed party staged at a Bedfordshire airfield was a night to remember. With hundreds of staff attending, I realised that we were no longer a small company. With operational staff and crew now based away from easyLand, the parties were the only place where all the easyJet family could get together. This wasn't just about indulgence and staff letting their hair down, it had become a part of our organisational culture. You might think that partying at easyJet was no different from British Airways, but we seemed to have a magic ingredient - and sometimes there could be unanticipated business benefits.

In early 1996, we'd decided to throw a staff party at Luton. The exact cause of celebration escapes me now (in fact, we didn't always need a reason!). As was often the case, invitations were extended to local business partners, such as suppliers and airport handling staff. What was different on this occasion was that one particular farsighted individual had invited a contingent of baggage handlers down from the Scottish airports, even flying them down to the party free of charge. With the party in full swing, I spoke to a burly baggage handler who told me in a broad Glaswegian accent and in no uncertain terms that this was the first time any airline had invited "the likes of them" to a party. Baggage handlers had something of a reputation for militancy, but on this occasion the decision to invite them proved to be an inspired one. Indeed, I'm convinced that in the weeks following the party, baggage from easyJet flights flew off the airport conveyor belts more rapidly than those of our competitors.

Although a lot of planning and original thinking had gone into the business plan, market research at least in the conventional sense played a relatively small part in easyJet's creation and development. Rather than rely on what market researchers told him about his customers, Stelios placed great store on listening to passengers on board the flights he took. He'd often bring their feedback with him to the marketing meetings. Not only was this faster than research, it was a lot cheaper too.

In 1999 easyGroup opened the world's largest internet café on Wilton Road near London's Victoria Station. In keeping with our low-cost philosophy, we decided to have no background music in the store. There was a simple public address system, but no facility to pipe music to our customers. Soon after opening, it became apparent that the sound of several hundred people simultaneously tapping, coughing and chatting on their mobile phones was, at best, distracting. Consequently, when we fitted out our second and even bigger, five-hundred-seat internet café on London's Tottenham Court Road, we took the precaution of installing a music system while a debate raged as to whether our customers really wanted background music. I suggested a programme of market research, but Stelios had a better idea. One November evening a few weeks after opening, the store was full (picture five hundred people huddled over PCs, tapping away) as Stelios switched on the shop's public-address system. "Hi, I'm Stelios and I own this place," he announced. A few dozen people looked up to see what was behind this unprompted interruption to their surfing. Stelios continued: "We've been having some discussions about whether we should have music in our stores. .. ." a ragged cheer went up "...and I've decided to ask you myself. So, would everyone who wants to hear music please put up their hand?" Instantly, around four hundred hands shot into the air. Without further ceremony, Stelios pressed a switch and music filled the air. The quickest, most direct and certainly the cheapest market-research study I've ever witnessed.

In 1998, Stelios took another bold decision when he allowed television cameras into easyJet to film a "fly on the wall" documentary series. The first series of "Airline" to feature the budget airline aired on ITV in January 1999 and was an instant hit, attracting audiences of up to ten million viewers. The public, it seemed, was captivated by the sight of fuming passengers dealing with delays, lost baggage and the hundred and one things that can possibly go wrong at an airport. Giving the cameras unfettered, behind-the-scenes access to their operations in this way would have been inconceivable to most companies. In easyJet's case, it was a calculated gamble, typical of Stelios' bold style that gave the airline an unprecedented level of brand awareness - not just in the UK, but also in many overseas markets where the documentary has subsequently aired. Some sceptics contend that to show easyJet passengers going through travel-related traumas casts the airline in a negative light. In my view, most people understand that "passenger shows up, checks in and arrives on time after an uneventful flight" doesn't make for great television.

Saving money wasn't the only consideration in our ongoing efforts to do things differently. We were also aware that our customers wanted to understand how easyJet was able to offer lower fares without compromising safety. There are many differences between the business models of a low-cost and a full-service airline that collectively account for the price differential. From a marketing standpoint, we focussed on three that the public found it easy to understand: cutting out the travel agent, using Luton rather than Heathrow and having no meal on board the plane. These were developed into key themes used in our early advertising campaigns. Coupled with a strategy of showing our modern fleet of aircraft, this appeared to reassure customers that we were saving money by cutting out the things they didn't need rather than compromising their safety.

The choice of Luton - considered back then to be a charter airport - as the base for a new scheduled airline was unconventional, but turned out to be an inspired decision. Most passengers automatically assumed the Bedfordshire airport was cheaper than Heathrow, but it was less immediately apparent that it also afforded better punctuality. All other things being equal, the lower number of flights gave an airline based at Luton a time-keeping advantage over an airline operating out of congested Heathrow. With the business traveller in mind, we highlighted the differences in a string of press ads that compared the punctuality of airlines operating from the two airports. Inevitably, this advantage has been eroded over time, and I doubt the comparison would look quite so favourable today.

But the punctuality edge was an added bonus: the real reason we'd come to Luton was the low airport charges on offer. The original deal struck in 1995 had been favourable to easyJet but, like all good things, some day it was going to come to an end. In 1998, the authorities at Luton airport announced their intention to construct a new terminal building to provide much needed additional capacity. In the three years since easyJet's arrival, passenger numbers had more than doubled from 1.8 million to over 4 million a year. Further substantial growth in passengers was anticipated, and something had to be done to accommodate them.

The new building was to be no ordinary airport terminal, but a state-of-the-art facility designed by no less than the multi-award-winning architect, Sir Norman Foster. To put it mildly, easyJet was concerned by the prospect of such extravagance. While the airline acknowledged the need to upgrade the airport infrastructure, it sought a more functional facility designed to cater for the smooth and efficient processing of millions of low-cost passengers. What you want is an "easyShed" said one of Luton airport's managers disparagingly in an unguarded moment. That's exactly what we want, I thought to myself.

The main problem with Luton's proposal was that any spectacular, gleaming glass cathedral would have to be paid for out of the pockets of the passengers using the airport. By now, a large and increasing proportion of these passengers was flying with easyJet. In revitalising Luton, we had become victims of our own success. The battle to stop the development of what Stelios took to calling "The Taj Mahal" was fought largely behind the scenes for the next year and a half. But things flared up dramatically in early 1999 with the entry onto the scene of Barclays bank as a leading member of a consortium providing the development financing. It was rumoured that the new consortium intended to raise landing fees by some 300%, an increase that would significantly impact our profitability. Meanwhile, construction work was continuing apace and, in November 1999, the new passenger terminal was opened by Prince Philip and Her Majesty The Queen. The official ceremony was boycotted by easyJet in protest at what it called "an airport management hell-bent on wrecking Luton airport and returning it to the days of Lorraine Chase".

For easyJet, the involvement of Barclays lent a silver lining to this particular cloud. The bank provided a far more appropriate target for a "David versus Goliath" campaign than Luton airport, which was difficult to cast in the role of an 800-pound Gorilla. Stelios personally led the campaign, cutting up his own Barclaycard and a giant cardboard version during a protest outside the banking giant's Luton branch in June 2000. Naturally enough, the TV cameras were in attendance. The strength of feeling on the issue was evident in a statement released on the airline's website that ran "Barclays Bank is obviously not content with closing rural branches, charging for cashpoint withdrawals and granting its fat-cat bosses huge salaries and bonuses. It is now trying to milk easyJet passengers." This wasn't just a war of words: by now, easyJet had established a second UK base at Liverpool and was able to increase the pressure by adding new capacity in the north west, rather than at its spiritual home. It was suggested that if no new deal could be agreed then all future expansion would go to other airports. Upping the stakes further, Stelios wrote to John Prescott and called for Luton to be regulated in the same way as the other major London airports. Perhaps wisely, the Government elected to stay out of the row, saying merely that pricing was a matter between the airport and its customers.

Eventually, an agreement (of sorts) was reached with the owners of Luton airport, but it was far from being an easyJet victory. In February 2001, Barclays cashed out, selling its 65% share in Luton to airport operator TBI for an undisclosed price, said to be in the region of £82 million. On the day of the transfer, as the bank headed for the exit with its bag of cash, easyJet was chasing it down the road to get some of it back. The airline sent Barclays a £700,000 invoice to compensate for what it termed "a totally unnecessary closure of the airport" following bad weather. According to a statement on easyJet's website, the closure was a result of the bank's "underinvestment in airport services and poor corporate governance that accompanied its 20 months in control at the airport."

It would take some time for the dust to finally settle. Despite the change in ownership, bitterness lingered. A "Barclays Fat Cat Charge" of £5.50, imposed by easyJet on Luton-departing passengers, remained for many months afterwards. The battles with the bank and the airport's management had failed to prevent a steep rise in charges, but it would be untrue to say the campaign had achieved nothing. Once again, Stelios had secured acres of PR coverage and reinforced easyJet's positioning as a brand that fights for the interest of customers. The conflict with Luton had spurred expansion at Liverpool and on the continent, where the long-term opportunities for expansion were greater. In the final analysis, the bold decision in 1995 to base the airline at Luton was vindicated by the spectacular growth that resulted. The eventual hike in airport charges was simply a price for success that would one day have to be paid.

Incorporating fresh thinking when you're starting a new business clearly makes sense, but in the long term nearly every new idea can be copied. Standing still simply isn't an option in an industry as fast moving as civil aviation - and even 800-pound Gorillas eventually wake up and smell the coffee. The list of easyJet "firsts" is a long one. Many of them delivered some degree of short-term competitive advantage, others failed and were dropped, most of those that worked were copied by competitors. What really counted, more than any individual new idea, was that we managed to develop a culture of innovation and were always open to new ways of thinking. I believe this was a significant achievement that would serve easyJet well in future years, and prove to be a foundation stone of the airline's long-term success.

Technology takes off

Quote: "I think there's a market for maybe five computers in the world." (IBM President in 1943)

I'd seen enough in my time at British Airways understand that technology is a sword that potentially cuts both ways. Nearly all new technologies are available to both incumbents and new entrants, but for existing operators there is always the issue of how to deal with the issues of legacy systems and existing business processes. An example of this was the signific ant sums of money spent by British Airways on reservations and distribution technology in the late 80s and early 90s. This had allowed the airline to get itself in prime position onto the computer screens of tens of thousands of travel agents around the world. But times were changing. The shift in power from travel agents to travellers, coupled with the relentless march of the internet, made the wisdom of such investments look increasingly questionable.

Anyone launching a new business has the advantage of starting with a blank sheet of paper when it comes to deploying technology to maximum effect. This didn't need to be explained to Stelios who was a natural technophile; not that he always wanted the latest and greatest gadget, but he did have a passion for any application of technology that might aid efficiency in the workplace. At my job interview, he spoke at some length of the paperless office environment named *Keyfile* he had successfully introduced at his shipping company, Stelmar, and of his intention to do the same at easyJet. Under *Keyfile*, every document, fax (and, eventually, email) coming into the airline was optically scanned and categorised according to key words through which it could be searched for and retrieved.

A key principle behind the *Keyfile* philosophy was that information was of maximum value when shared and accessible by all. Consequently, in our first few months at Luton the paperless office was implemented in its purest form. All employees with a *Keyfile* login had access to every document held within the airline. This inevitably gave rise to some problems, particularly when it came to finding out how much everyone got paid. It was fascinating being part of what I thought of as an experiment in information and human behaviour, though it was probably never sustainable - particularly in light of the raft of data-protection legislation that has emerged in recent years.

There was no more ruthless practitioner of the paperless office environment than Stelios himself. If he spotted paper on your desk, it would be swept unceremoniously into a large plastic bin with "scan everything" written in large letters on the side. As Marketing Director, I received large quantities of promotional mail, much of it in funny shapes and sizes that weren't easily scanned. But there were to be no exceptions to the rule, and I only learnt my lesson when, for the third time, my desk was swept clear on one of the marauding Chairman's paper patrols.

Nick Manoudakis, easyJet's Finance Director, kept a hidden stash of documents in the ladies' toilets. I often wondered what female visitors to our offices using the facility thought the filing cabinets were doing there. The reason was that this was the only place in easyLand where they were safe from Stelios' mission to rid the office of paper. The fact that Nick's wife was easyJet's office manager meant that documents could be safely retrieved when required without questions being asked of Nick's use of the ladies' convenience. In the main, the filing cabinets contained invoices and VAT documents, giving rise to inevitable jokes (carefully whispered out of Stelios' earshot) about being flush with cash and the need to spend a penny.

When the decision was taken to build easyJet's first website back in 1997, no one could have foreseen the impact that the internet was to have on the airline's future. Stelios himself was initially sceptical, begrudgingly approving a limited budget for the site. "The internet is for geeks and nerds," he told us. To be honest I shared our Chairman's scepticism, but MD Ray Webster was an enthusiastic backer of the project and that swung the decision. Working initially with Tableau, a small Hertfordshire-based agency, we created a site which didn't allow online booking, but featured a unique telephone number that appeared on the website - and nowhere else. Consequently, we were able to attribute calls coming in on that number as having originated from the website. The volume of calls resulting from this internet presence was sufficiently large to justify the further investment required to develop an online booking capability, and easyJet's march on the road to becoming the self-styled "web's favourite airline" had begun. In April 1998, the easyJet online booking system went live, with around thirty bookings being made on the first day. A couple of months later, when the percentage of business coming in via the internet was in the low single digits, Stelios told me he expected to hit at least 50% by the end of the following year. I thought he was crazy and told him so: I just couldn't imagine that the internet would ever be the preferred booking channel for our mainstream customers. The reality was that our customers were taking to online booking like a duck takes to water. I hadn't appreciated that the whole transaction process is far easier for the customer to manage when he or she is doing it themselves. On a computer screen, we could display not only the prices for the customer's first choice of flights but also different alternatives, allowing passengers to make their own trade-offs between dates and prices. We'd lowered our costs by outsourcing to the customers - and the customers loved it!

In the end, the Chairman's "crazy" target was comfortably exceeded - not just because the number of people using the web was taking off, but also because Stelios started taking decisions consistent with the stretching target he had set us. A good example was the decision to release the new schedule on the internet before the telephone. The move initially provoked a backlash from a segment of our passengers, but we held our nerve and the protests subsided. Another bold decision followed when Stelios elected to go further, offering a £5 discount to passengers booking via the web. This accelerated the migration online, something remarkable and unprecedented was happening. Belatedly other players in the European airline business, including British Airways, had started to wake up and develop their own web capabilities. But easyJet had the advantage of a big head-start on its competition. A major milestone was passed in July 2001 when "the web's favourite airline" sold its ten millionth seat through its website, comfortably outstripping all its online rivals. The growth in the airline's online sales gave rise to further financial benefits. While easyJet was experiencing years of high double-digit growth, the size of the Luton call centre remained broadly static. Without the internet, we would have had to build several additional centres to offer the booking capability that the airline's growth demanded.

Even at this early stage, the web opened up new opportunities to tweak British Airways' tail – and, naturally, easyJet took full advantage. The airline ran online competitions to suggest alternative names for the venture and to predict Go's financial losses in its first year of operation. The competitions attracted tens of thousands of entries, maintaining momentum and raising the profile of our ongoing campaign. We had discovered a powerful new weapon that allowed us to respond ever more rapidly to market developments and outwit competitors who were slow to realise the internet's true potential. We were starting to think about how this new weapon might be used against us. As a precautionary measure, we purchased the URL "sleazyjet.com". Apparently, the term was becoming increasingly used by passengers experiencing flight delays, and we wanted to avoid someone using it to set up a complaint site.

I look back on that time as a period of transition: the old media world still wielded significant power, but the internet was starting to make its presence felt. The trick was to make the two work effectively together. For some time, traditional airlines, British Airways included, had used newspaper promotions as a means of shifting seats that would otherwise go unsold. These seats were heavily discounted and offered for sale well in advance of the travel period to avoid diluting revenue that would come to the airline anyway. Normally, an additional hurdle was imposed, such as the requirement to collect a set number of tokens printed in the newspaper over a period of time. What easyJet did to the world of newspaper flight promotions was to supersize it, offering large volumes of off-peak seats at rock-bottom prices that made other travel offers look pathetic by comparison.

In true tabloid style, such promotions were invariably hyped as "The world's greatest flight offer". In reality, however, they tended to be pretty similar when the hype was stripped away. These special promotions, though phenomenally successful at shifting seats, gave rise to significant fulfilment problems due to the limited capacity of the easyJet call centre. In 1996, we ran a series of promotions with the *Daily Mirror* and its sister title, *Sunday Mirror*. Each promotion was bigger than the last, eventually culminating in what we called "The mother of all promotions". This time, we had overreached ourselves - the tabloids were in the middle of a vicious circulation battle and the *Mirror* had backed the promotion with substantial TV support. Undeterred by an extended token collection period, a tidal wave of readers hit the easyJet phone lines immediately they opened.

In a four-day promotional period, a BT contact estimated we were offered over four million calls at a time when we typically had around a hundred call-centre staff on duty. I spent much of the four days hiding from John MacLeod, easyJet's call-centre manager, dodging abuse from senior management at *Mirror Newspapers*. The atmosphere on the phones was feverish. One telephone agent told me of the call he'd just taken: "The guy had been waiting for hours to get through and was gibbering like a madman when he finally spoke to me. He said he wanted to fly to Nice. I told him all the Nice seats had gone. Then he said he wanted to fly to Barcelona, and when I told him all the Barcelona seats had sold out too, he said he wanted to fly to any place at any time. I ended up selling him two seats from Luton to Aberdeen in the middle of February. The next day he called me back and said I'd tricked him into buying them, and that he wanted his money back".

Just when it looked like these types of newspaper-fuelled promotions would collapse under the weight of their own success, the internet came riding to the rescue. Mandating internet booking as a condition of such promotions meant that many thousands of transactions could be handled simultaneously. I breathed a sigh of relief: the customer service backlash from our wave of promotions had been giving me some sleepless nights.

Maximising revenue by matching supply and demand is critical to all airlines but has particular relevance for low-cost carriers operating on wafer-thin margins. In order to understand how the likes of easyJet and Ryanair can make a profit on a £29 fare to the south of France while BA makes a loss, one needs to know the difference between fixed and marginal costs. The costs associated with carrying an additional passenger from Luton to Nice on an easyJet plane that was, say, already 70%

full were negligible. For a traditional airline, the marginal costs back in the late 90s included a meal or snack, travel-agent commission, reservations-systems costs plus the costs of printing and accounting for the physical ticket. The new breed of low-cost airlines could avoid all these expenses, allowing them to sell incremental seats for next to nothing. With the extra revenue flowing directly to the bottom line, it was - in theory at least - a finance director's dream. Not only that: each incremental passenger, regardless of the fare paid, could be sold products and services ranging from car hire and hotels to travel insurance and scratch cards.

It is important to note, however, that this is very different from saying that an airline can make a profit by flying a full plane load of passengers to the same destination, all paying £29. The viability of the whole model relies on there being a proportion of passengers willing to pay higher fares to travel at the times they want. Business travellers typically fall into this category. Sports fans and families with children tied to school holidays are other examples. Matching supply and demand through variable pricing is known in the airline business as "yield management". At most carriers, British Airways included, maximising revenue in this way was something of a black art. A typical yield-management system has behind it a complex series of algorithms which predict how full a flight is likely to end up based on historical performance and current rate of sale. At the time of our launch, easyJet's yield-management system was extremely crude, and we had no history of bookings on which to forecast future sales. A visitor to our offices might find Nick or myself huddled with Stelios over a PC, going through flights which looked to be selling too fast or too slow and adjusting the pricing accordingly. This was just about sustainable when we had a handful of routes, but wasn't a long-term solution. We were leaving a lot of money on the table. This was recognised by revenue-management whizz-kid, John Stephenson, and MD Ray Webster who'd joined easyJet with a wealth of pricing experience from Air New Zealand. Together, they brought a more rigorous and automated approach to yield management that unlocked significant extra revenue and delivered a marked increase in profitability. Within easyJet today, as for all airlines of any size, yield management has become highly computerised and the pricing algorithms are the stuff of rocket scientists.

Undeniably, technology was among the key drivers of easyJet's early year's success. It helped that we had one of the coolest, cleverest and most laid-back IT teams in the airline business (Clive, Kerry and Trevor: take a bow). These guys weren't locked away in some windowless basement with just each other and pizza boxes for company. Instead, they were seated right next to the call centre at the very heart of the business. If easyJet's booking system or the telephones went down, they would know about it immediately. On one occasion, I was made aware of a computer problem by the sound of a hundred people shouting "Trevor!" at the tops of their voices. In our first year, when sales agents were paid exclusively on the number of seats sold, you can imagine the pressure that the easyJet IT team was under to get problems fixed quickly!

When it came to technology, fortune smiled on us yet again. The coming of age of the internet could hardly have been better timed. But although luck and having the right people were undeniably important, in truth it was Stelios' readiness to experiment and his evangelism for technology-driven change that really made the difference.

Today, the application of technology impacts on easyJet's passengers at every stage of their journey. From online booking and texted confirmations to flight changes, self-service check-in and printing of boarding passes; even complaint handling and refunds are largely automated. I doubt whether even Stelios could have foreseen the huge role that technology has played in reshaping the industry and in turbo-charging the growth of his airline.

Smells like team spirit

"If the employees come first then they're happy,...a motivated employee treats the customers well. The customer is happy so they keep coming back...it's just the way it works." (Herb Kelleher)

I've long held that success in any service business depends in large measure on the quality and motivation of the people who work for it, particularly those in customer-facing roles. Testimony to this belief can be found in the focus on employees at Southwest Airlines who proudly state that, in their business, customers come second to staff. For the Dallas based carrier these weren't just empty words. Not only was Southwest consistently profitable and the winner of countless customer-service awards, the airline also enjoyed a reputation for having a loyal, close-knit and highly motivated workforce.

Southwest's achievement was all the more remarkable given the airline's size, geographic distribution and rapid growth. On the journey from struggling start-up to large successful multinational, organisations invariably lose something of the team spirit that makes small companies much better places to work in. For me, a key turning point at easyJet came when we reached a size that meant I no longer knew the name of everyone in the office. Fighting against the drift towards de-personalisation, Southwest had somehow managed to preserve the small-company culture that made it a great business to work for in the eyes of its employees and their peers. In marked contrast, I'd seen at first hand the corrosive effects of poor employee relations during my time with British Airways. This was one area where I was confident we could secure a distinct advantage over our Gorilla opponents.

Southwest place great store by their considered recruitment process. Their recruitment philosophy can be summed up in the often quoted mantra "Hire for attitude, train for skills". Having taken this very much to heart, in our initial recruitment for sales staff, I set about finding individuals who were energetic and enthusiastic rather than experienced telephone salespeople. We'd managed to find the people we wanted, with around sixty applicants for the twenty positions available. As time went on and the date of our first flight got closer, word started to spread that easyJet was a serious and well-funded venture. It became apparent we'd need to find a way of dealing with the vast numbers of people who wanted to come and work for us.

Back in the mid 90s, Luton was something of an unemployment black spot. Local people were always alert to new employers, particularly if they were based at the airport. Even so, when we put out a message on the local radio station inviting applications for positions as cabin crew and telesales agents, we were unprepared for the scale of the response. Those interested were invited to come to easyLand on one of a number of scheduled open evenings. At the first such event, a queue of around two hundred hopefuls had formed outside easyLand by the time the doors opened. After registering at reception, the candidates were funnelled through a hallway where Stelios, Dave

McCulloch (our Operations Director) and myself sat behind a large desk. With so many applicants to get through, each "interview" lasted less than three minutes. We asked them two questions chosen at random from a list of half a dozen and, based on hand signals, indicated to one another whether we felt they should be invited back for a second interview. By the time the last applicant had gone home, not only was it close to midnight: it was also clear that we wouldn't have a recruitment problem for frontline staff. Even at its less glamorous end, the allure of the airline business ensured a seemingly limitless supply of capable recruits.

With employee numbers growing, we worked hard to replicate Southwest's successful people-oriented formula. An internal "culture group" was set up with elected representatives from different departments. Led by Chris Goscomb, this team was charged with maintaining a strong company culture as easyJet continued its relentless expansion. Copies of "Nuts", the best-selling story of Southwest's success, were given out to managers, and at one point a couple of groups (including myself) were sent off to Dallas on week-long study tours to watch and learn from the masters. Rather than shroud their successful people formula in secrecy, Southwest operated an open-door policy to airlines from around the world.

One of the most significant ideas to be implemented following our return from the United

States, was the regular after work barbecue. Admittedly, the climate in Luton was a few degrees cooler than in Texas, but we improvised by erecting a small marquee outside easyLand. With food and drink provided by the company, the barbecue was open to all easyJet employees and took place every Friday between 6 and 8 p.m. Stelios would sometimes be found manning the barbecue. Although an enthusiastic chef who looked the part, he wasn't as good at cooking sausages as he was running an airline. It was a great opportunity for easyJet's operational and commercial staff to mingle informally, provide feedback from customers and swap ideas.

It's fair to say that not all the ideas we brought back from Southwest were as successful as the Friday barbecue. One which definitely "failed to translate" was the easyJet "recognition ceremony". This involved employees who had delivered over and above the call of duty being acknowledged in an easyLand ceremony during which they were applauded and cheered by the assembled airline staff. This much-ridiculed event became known as "getting the clap". Indeed, persistent giggling from more juvenile elements in the marketing department led to it being quietly dropped.

In the period leading up to the launch of easyJet's first international service to Amsterdam in the spring of 1996, we considered carefully our options for handling calls from the Dutch public. Initial research suggested we would struggle to find sufficient Dutch speakers within commuting distance of Luton airport. Furthermore, at that time we were neither sufficiently well known nor paying enough to attract applications from further afield. We therefore approached a large call-handling centre near Amsterdam which agreed to field calls from our Dutch customers on a flat-fee basis charged every time a booking was made. The arrangement worked well enough, but was proving expensive: on average, it cost three times as much to handle a call from a Dutch customer as it did their English counterpart. Then, one day, on a routine visit to the Amsterdam call centre, we were listening into calls when the penny dropped. The majority of calls between Dutch agents and Dutch customers were actually taking place in English! Within a few months, we had terminated our relationship with the Dutch call centre and were handling calls in English from easyLand. A small team of native Dutch speakers were retained in customer-service roles. This was because the Dutch people had a tendency to revert to their native language when making a complaint.

In the early years, although easyJet offered no discounted travel to its employees, staff did enjoy a more unusual fringe benefit. The airline was now running regular PR stunts in the UK and overseas, and employees were often able to participate. In October 1998, easyJet organised a famous trip to Brussels where Stelios was to hold a meeting with European Competition officials. We had lodged an official complaint against British Airways, alleging cross-subsidisation of their low-cost airline, Go. As always, we looked at how we could make our point in style. We flew out to the Belgian capital on a specially prepared easyJet aircraft with "Stop BA, Stop Go" emblazoned in large letters on the side.

This time, we had over a hundred orange boiler-suited staff, family and friends along for the ride. The visual impact on the streets of Brussels was extraordinary, making for more great media coverage and further building the brand. The European Competition Authorities (ECA) listened politely as Stelios argued his case forcefully in front of them. But he took so long to emerge from their offices that I was forced to negotiate an increase in my credit-card limit to pay the lunch bill for one hundred and fifty hungry people in Brussels. Even though the officials decided not to intervene, the event was judged to have been a success. We'd made our point, the trip more than covered its cost in PR terms and the staff and their families had a great day out.

As anyone who's ever watched the "Airline" series on TV can testify, coping with the unexpected goes with the territory when you're working for an airline. Nevertheless, easyJet seemed to get more than its fair share of customer-service challenges in its first twelve months. It took some time for all our planes and pilots to be fully equipped and trained with "category three" capability allowing landing in conditions of poor visibility. Located at the top of a hill, Luton was particularly susceptible to fog. As a result, we were sometimes forced to divert flights to other airports in the Midlands and beyond. Having personally experienced the ordeal of a long coach ride back to Luton, my true identity unknown to passengers muttering darkly about management incompetence, I was well aware of the reputational damage such disruption could cause. Thankfully, instances like the infamous occasion in the late 90s when a freak weather pattern caused it to snow at Luton airport but nowhere else in the country were rare. Along with other senior managers, I was sometimes thrown into the front line to deal with angry customers facing long delays to their journeys. For those of us who had no background in handling such situations, it was quite an experience.

In October 1996, there was a memorable incident involving a planeload of passengers who had been stranded at Luton by a bout of severe weather. The disgruntled travellers had been informed that they wouldn't be going anywhere until the following day. I was working late in easyLand that evening when word came in from our handling staff in the terminal that the passengers were on the brink of rioting. It was snowing heavily, so I put on my boots and winter coat and walked the short distance from our offices to the airport terminal to check out the situation for myself. As I walked through the entry doors with my pass around my neck, a couple of hefty policemen who were walking out said "Good luck, son". My efforts to placate the passengers failed miserably, and I beat a hasty retreat to easyLand where I phoned Stelios who was at his home in Monaco. Stelios told me to call the Finance Director at his home, get him to come into the office and give each of the stranded customers £100. Nick was unhappy, not at being called into the office so late, but with the idea of giving refunds. His mood worsened when he discovered there weren't enough cheques in the company chequebook to meet the boss's request. Somehow, word had got through to the passengers that their demand for compensation was being met, but I was sure things would turn ugly again if we didn't deliver. Down the line from Monaco came our instructions: if we didn't have enough cheques then we should pay them cash. Nick exploded, "Where the hell does he think I'm going to get £10,000 at this time on a Friday night?" To Nick's credit, he managed to persuade the Thomas Cook bureau de change in the airport terminal to lend us the cash, which we duly stuffed into a briefcase. With the biggest call-centre agent I could find standing guard, the passengers formed an orderly queue to collect their £100.

Stelios certainly enjoyed a good rapport with the airline's frontline staff, but there was more to easyJet's people-orientated culture than the leadership of a charismatic chairman. For me, there was one particular incident that demonstrated more than any other the team spirit of the young airline and our ability to rise to a challenge. It happened in April 1997 when a series of bomb threats resulted in the sudden closure of the Luton airport terminal building. Chaos ensued, with passengers turning up for their flights but unable to enter the terminal. Fortunately, easyLand backed onto one of the airport taxiways and we were given approval to depart passengers from our offices directly onto the planes lined up outside (difficult to imagine in today's security-fixated world). Announcements went out via the travel desks of local radio stations that easyJet would do its best to get all passengers to their destinations. Our offices were a hive of activity with our "never-say-die" ops managers, Lisa Roblin and Jane Horton, in the thick of things. To me, easyLand resembled a giant *Blue Peter* set with makeshift cardboard signs indicating destinations fastened with sellotape above office desks set up as rudimentary check-ins. Announcements were made through a hand-held megaphone and our office vending machines did a roaring trade. Staff on their days off heard what was going on and phoned in to help out. In short, everyone pulled together. We were the only airline to operate from Luton that day and, amazingly, easyJet was able to depart over a thousand passengers who otherwise would have been unable to travel. Thankfully, the spate of bomb threats ended soon after and airport operations returned to normal. No one who played a part in that very special day will ever forget it. The airline's investment in its people and company culture had been repaid handsomely. Gorilla, eat your heart out!

Today, with many thousands of staff across many different countries and cultures, easyJet faces significant challenges in managing its people - the kind of challenges facing most large multinational companies in a fast-moving customer-service business. From an outsider's perspective, the airline doesn't look or feel like a European "Southwest". Perhaps it was never realistic to think the people-oriented culture developed and nurtured in the company's start-up could be sustained over such a long period? Yet, to me and to many of those working at easyJet during those early years, it felt like we were part of something very special indeed.

Take me to your leader

"Stelios is easyJet, easyJet is Stelios." (Robert Ayling, British Airways CEO)

Whenever people ask me about my time with easyJet and the easyGroup, the most common line of questioning surrounds Stelios himself. What's he like to work for? What makes him tick? These aren't easy questions to answer, even after five years working for the guy. Where do I begin?

I first met Stelios in the spring of 1995 at a small restaurant in Mayfair's Shepherd Market. The meeting had been set up by Norman Broadbent, a London-based headhunting firm who'd been appointed to find a Sales and Marketing Director for the start-up airline. I'd already been interviewed by easyJet's acting MD, Peter Leishman, but this was to be the key meeting. There was no Google back then, but I'd done enough homework to know that Stelios came from a wealthy shipping background, that he was a graduate of the City Business School and that he'd already set up a successful shipping company of his own. He was four years younger than me, thick set with the presence and confidence of someone much older than his years. I felt the interview was going well - he was friendly, but the questioning was direct and incisive. Stelios asked a lot of questions about my time with British Airways and Thomas Cook. What could I bring to easyJet? When I described myself as a potential "gamekeeper turned poacher", he seemed to find this amusing. We carried on chatting over lunch. I was impressed. Stelios was smart, articulate and ambitious, and the vision he painted for the airline was compelling. By the time we got to the coffee, I'd made my mind up: if he offered me the job, I'd take it. Interview over, I got in my car and began the drive back to

Peterborough where I then lived. Half-way up the A1, the phone rang. I turned the car around and headed back to London. I'd just become easyJet's third employee.

There could be no questioning the guy's drive and commitment. Stelios only knew one way to lead - and that was from the front. The only person he drove harder than his management team was himself. Of course, this was no rags-to-riches tale. By most standards, Stelios was already hugely wealthy - with fast cars, a speedboat and a penthouse apartment in Monaco. Yet, for a while at least, he was prepared to give up this lifestyle to work in a tin shack in Luton, often into the small hours, before heading off to the local Ibis hotel for a few hours' shuteye. As ever, Stelios had an eye for a bargain. When we first set up base in Luton, he initially stayed at the three-star Strathmore Hotel in the town centre, but had no hesitation in downgrading when he found the two-star Ibis to be cheaper.

The airline's founder had none of the airs and graces you might expect from someone born with a silver spoon (more like a platinum ladle) in their mouth. One afternoon, he was showing a group of important-looking visitors around easyLand (investment bankers, possibly). Opening a can of diet coke from the vending machine, it sprayed a shower of sticky brown liquid in all directions. Unabashed, Stelios trotted off to the toilets. Returning with a roll of paper, he got down on his knees and started mopping the floor. The smartly dressed visitors looked on in disbelief at Stelios as he pronounced "at easyJet, we clean up our own mess". His "roll-your-sleeves-up" attitude, approachability and easy-going manner greatly endeared Stelios to the airline's junior staff, particularly those working in the call centre some of whom hero worshipped him.

Throughout the early growth years, Stelios remained alert to the views of another critically important constituency: the pilots. In my opinion, there are two key reasons why all airlines need to stay close to their pilots. Not only are they the one group of employees that can bring operations to a grinding halt through industrial action, they also talk to their colleagues and fellow pilots from other airlines, providing a vital source of insight and information. Pre-9/11, when security rules permitted, easyJet's Chairman often sat up front in the cockpit with the pilots. We were a small business, and because Stelios was flying frequently he quickly became attuned to the pilots' views on how his airline was being run.

For the senior management of the airline, particularly those on the start-up team, the relationship with Stelios was different. The start-up phase of easyJet was a tough working environment, particularly for those of us with young families. Like most entrepreneurs starting a new business, Stelios demanded a lot, with managers expected to make substantial personal sacrifices. Holidays were at the then legal minimum of fifteen days per year; leave of more than five days in a row was frowned upon. The workload was unrelenting. When we were in start-up mode, six-day weeks were the norm and our Chairman - unburdened by parental responsibilities - led by example. The management team knew that Stelios could be difficult, particularly when he was under pressure. A strong camaraderie developed between us, and we supported one another when times were tough. The worst moment was when our operations director, Dave McCulloch, died suddenly and unexpectedly. Dave was a true professional, much respected in the industry. He had played a critical role in getting easyJet off the ground. It was a sobering moment but, if anything, his death brought us even closer together. There wasn't much time to reflect - we were fighting to establish the airline, and Stelios was pushing us hard. The start-up team thrived on the adrenaline. Despite the workload and the high stress levels, we were all there willingly. I felt more productive than at any point in my working life.

Remarkably for a man so often in the public eye, Stelios managed to keep his private life out of the media. From the earliest days of easyJet, he maintained a clear distinction between his business and personal affairs, with the two worlds seldom overlapping. One exception was the party he traditionally held at his Monaco apartment during the Formula One Grand Prix. This was one of the few times you got to see Stelios among his friends. Invitations to this particular party were much sought-after, for his apartment overlooked the harbour and afforded spectacular views of the racing circuit. Even at these events, there were few clues to the private side of his life: I never saw him with a partner of any kind, and his friends were tight-lipped when it came to discussing personal relationships.

Although Stelios could lay claim to being the man who brought low-cost air fares to the British public, there are other pretenders to that particular crown. For me, the true budget airline pioneer was Sir Freddie Laker whose transatlantic Skytrain had been forced out of business by British Airways many years earlier. I'd followed the story of Laker as a child and, through Stelios, one morning at a hotel near Victoria Station I finally got to meet the man who'd proved to be such a thorn in the side of British Airways. As I listened to the two airline pioneers chatting in animated fashion over breakfast, it was apparent that they had much in common. Nevertheless, I was also struck by the contrast between the two men. To my mind, Laker was a laid-back aviation buccaneer from a different age where aviation still carried with it romantic associations. Stelios, meanwhile, was very much the hard-nosed calculating young businessman, single-minded, totally focussed and hungry for success.

One characteristic the two men shared was a tendency to recourse to law when threatened. Freddie Laker's catchphrase "sue the bastards" was an expression that Stelios adopted with relish, with his penchant for litigation set to become something of a trademark over the next few years. Indeed, I lost count of the number of legal threats or actions easyJet initiated during my time with them. In the first hectic few months, it seemed we were in almost daily contact with Hugh O'Donovan, a sharp but genial lawyer with London firm Wilde Sapte. What initially puzzled me was how often Stelios would request (and pay for) expensive legal advice which he then chose to ignore. It took me a while to realise that commencing legal proceedings could often be looked upon as a sound promotional investment, regardless of the eventual outcome.

Of all the airline owners and bosses, the best-known among the public at large remains Sir Richard Branson. By the time easyJet took off, the founder of Virgin Atlantic and many other ventures was already a household name. His first move into the European low-cost sector came in 1996 when he bought the Belgian leisure airline, EBA. Based out of Brussels and rebranded as Virgin Express the airline operated a fleet of Boeing 737s flying mainly to destinations in southern Europe. Some speculated that Brussels was the wrong place to base a start-up; others that the Virgin brand didn't sit well with the low-cost sector. In any event, the airline failed to match the dramatic growth of easyJet or Ryanair and was eventually sold and merged with another Brussels-based carrier. Branson made his next low-cost play on the other side of the world. This time round, he was markedly more successful. In 2000, he established Virgin Blue, a low-cost carrier that would eventually become Australia's second-largest airline. Yet although he had "skin in the game", I suspected that it wasn't just the progress of a low-cost competitor that was attracting Branson's interest in easyJet. With his old enemy British Airways involved, he would almost certainly be watching with interest from afar as we slugged it out with the Gorilla.

I'd never met the man who BA's former Chairman, Lord King, once famously described as "the grinning pullover", but was well aware of his reputation and achievements. Stelios, though, had met Sir Richard a few years earlier when he briefly considered investing in a conventional airline franchise, an opportunity on which he chose to pass. In July 1998, their paths crossed again. Stelios, myself and easyJet's Eton-educated PR Head, James Rothnie, attended a lecture given by the bearded entrepreneur to BBC's *Money Programme* at its Television Centre in London. When the filming was over, we chatted to Branson in the BBC bar. Stelios invited him to a Greek restaurant near Tottenham Court Road. In this particular restaurant, customers were allowed to smash plates as long as they paid for what they broke. The night was a long one: Stelios and Branson seemed to get on like a house on fire. Rude messages for British Airways were scrawled on plates with a marker pen and dashed to the ground. It was childish, but great fun. Amid the festivities, one of the two remembered that our driver, Bob Vickers, was sitting outside in his car, so invited him to join us. At the end of the evening, the bill for broken plates was bigger than the bill for the actual meal. There was some animated discussion between the two multi-millionaires about who would pick up the tab (I can't recall who actually paid but it certainly wasn't me!). The evening had felt like a celebration and an acknowledgement of easyJet's achievements. It counted for a lot: Richard Branson wasn't just one of the country's most famous businessmen, he was the man with a reputation for running rings round the 800-pound Gorilla.

At the same time that Stelios was forging a reputation as one of the industry's more colourful personalities, another airline boss was starting to make his mark. Enter Michael O'Leary, Chief Executive of Ryanair. Like Stelios, he was quick-thinking, opinionated and ambitious - but that was where the similarities ended. It was true that Stelios could occasionally be quick tempered with his management team, but to employees in general and his customers in particular he was polite and charming. Rarely, if ever, did he swear. He would also avoid giving personal offence. By contrast, O'Leary appeared not to care whom he upset, his pronouncements and press conferences being peppered with bad language. Among the more colourful quotes ascribed to O'Leary is his infamous pronouncement: "What part of no refund don't you understand? You're not getting a refund, so f*** off!". Stelios was appalled by such behaviour. In general, he took a tough line on refunds, but if confronted by customers he would always explain the rationale behind the policy politely and patiently. On rare occasions, he was willing to exercise discretion if there was a genuine hardship case. Michael Skapinker, writing in the *Financial Times* reported how in the early days a customer had phoned demanding to speak to the airline's Chairman. The customer had booked his honeymoon with easyJet, but the wedding had been called off. After speaking to the prospective groom, Stelios relented offering a refund. The customer said that he didn't want a refund he just wanted to change the name of the person he was travelling with! The incident led to the creation of a new service: allowing passenger name changes - for a fee.

There can be no disputing the achievement of Michael O'Leary in transforming a struggling Irish carrier into one of the world's largest and most profitable airlines. But the means by which this has been achieved have been highly controversial. In the words of *The Economist*, Ryanair has managed to be both utterly successful and absolutely disliked. Safety and punctuality aside, Ryanair took cost-cutting to new levels by looking at every opportunity to lower fares. Their obsession with cost control made easyJet look profligate in comparison. It was rumoured that staff were banned from charging their mobile phones using the company electricity. The Irish airline showed that it could play the PR game, too. It issued headline-grabbing statements on proposals as diverse as extra charges for overweight customers, fees to use the toilets and even redesigned aircraft that allowed standing-room only. None of the initiatives outlined has actually come to pass, but invariably they have generated substantial press coverage for Ryanair, reinforcing its reputation as cost cutters *par excellence*.

The Irish airline also had a different but highly successful approach to choosing its routes. While easyJet focussed for the most part on destination airports in major cities, Ryanair would fly to secondary airports, often in places you'd never heard of with rock-bottom landing fees. In an early dig at its rival, easyJet ran some poster ads at Stansted with the strapline "fly to an airport, not an airfield". The sheer size of the European air market and the different approaches the two airlines were taking to selecting new routes allowed both to prosper. Minor skirmishing on the Glasgow route aside, the rivals managed to avoid potentially destructive head-to-head competition. At least in those early years we shared a common enemy in the shape of the British Airway's 800-pound Gorilla. But when the two airlines and their respective figureheads finally did cross swords, the sparks really began to fly.

To my eternal regret, I wasn't at easyJet in 2003 to witness the most famous and memorable Ryanair stunt. In a scene straight out of the pages of *"Boy's Own"*, Michael O'Leary dressed in battle fatigues drove a Sherman tank belching smoke to Luton airport on a mission to "liberate the public from easyJet's high fares". The tank's objective was the easyJet offices, but its progress was halted by airport security halfway up the hill leading to easyLand. Confined to the car park of the Holiday Inn Hotel, O'Leary and supporting Ryanair staff chanted slogans and sang uncomplimentary songs about their orange rival while the theme tune from *"The A-Team"* blared from loudspeakers. According to a report in *The Guardian,* the stunt was further hampered when an easyJet staff member removed the keys to the tank.

It was clear there was no love lost between the two men. The closest O'Leary ever got to paying a compliment to his Greek rival was to say: "He's the son of a billionaire. He could have been a rich tosser, but at least he started an airline." Years later, the personal animosity reached new levels when Ryanair ran an advertisement picturing Stelios as Pinocchio, calling on him to "stop hiding the truth" about easyJet's on-time performance. Predictably, Stelios went to his lawyers, contending the adverts were libellous. This move prompted further insults from O'Leary. The Irishman threw down a series of challenges to settle the dispute without recourse to lawyers. His initial proposal was a "chariots of fire" style race around Trafalgar Square. When this was turned down O'Leary suggested a Sumo-wrestling bout with him "supplying the nappies". But it was Stelios who emerged victorious when Ryanair was forced to apologise and pay the legal costs of easyJet's founder. Extracting an apology from Michael O'Leary is no mean feat, and Stelios placed advertisements of his own in the national press dedicating his victory to "all those members of the travelling public who have suffered verbal abuse and hidden extras at the hands of O'Leary".

Stelios is generally acknowledged to be an accomplished public speaker with an innate ability to handle the most difficult of interviewers. I have long believed that oratory is something you are born with; in my view, most airline bosses are poor speakers, including Richard Branson who understands the media and communications better than almost anyone. Stelios and Michael O'Leary, however, are naturals; never more at home than when in front of an audience or a television camera. I've lost count of the number of times I've seen Stelios with an audience in the palm of his hand and showing a remarkable ability to improvise.

One afternoon, I met Stelios - fresh back in London from a British Midland flight - at the QE2 Conference Centre in Westminster five minutes before he was due to deliver a scheduled conference speech. I broke the bad news that I'd forgotten to bring the CD containing his PowerPoint presentation, but instead of berating me he simply shrugged. Stepping onto the stage in front of an audience of over five hundred business people he took out of his pocket an apple and a Mars bar that together constituted the "meal" he'd been given on his flight. "Will anyone give me a tenner for this rubbish?" he bellowed, "Because that's what it costs British Midland to put it on the plane". The audience cheered, with some rising to their feet and applauding.

To say that Stelios had an eye for publicity is a bit like saying Leonardo Da Vinci was a dab hand with a pencil. A natural-born communicator, Stelios knew how to work the media to get what he wanted. Journalists loved his accessibility and outspokenness. On any subject relating to airlines, easyJet's Chairman could always be relied upon to have an opinion and come up with a good quote. He was certainly not above poking fun at himself if, in doing so, he could be sure of garnering a few column inches.

It was rare to catch Stelios off guard. Indeed, only once do I recall seeing him struggle to answer a journalist's question. The occasion was a scheduled interview with the *Scottish Daily Record* newspaper about the possibility of easyJet initiating direct services between Glasgow and European cities. Towards the end of the discussion, the journalist threw in the following question: "So, you started easyJet with a loan of five million pounds from your father, is that right?" Stelios: "yes". Reporter: "have you paid him back yet?" In truth, the rest of the Haji-Ioannou clan took little, if any, active part in running the business, even though his "football mad" brother, Polys, and sister, Clelia, both had substantial shareholdings in the airline. I rarely saw Clelia after easyJet's launch where she made a cameo appearance, but I did meet Polys on a number of (usually football-related) occasions. Stelios' older brother was a successful businessman in his own right, though he'd stayed in the shipping industry where Loucas, their father, had made his fortune. It was brought home to me just how wealthy the Haji-Ioannou family was when, in a rare but welcome diversion from the austerity of Luton, Polys invited me to accompany him to Monaco to watch a European Cup final. Of course, I'd be welcome to stay as a guest on his yacht! We flew down on easyJet together before being collected by a chauffeur-driven RollsRoyce. We had the best seats in the stadium. After the match, we ate with the players from both teams. And Stelios is giving this life up for Luton, I remember thinking to myself.

Naturally enough, Stelios was at the forefront when it came to planning and executing our PR stunts. With the boss leading the way, the rest of us were invariably up for it, and we pulled off many coups in those first crazy years. I can think of only one time where we chickened out. Someone - it might even have been Stelios - outlined a plan to drive down to Heathrow in a van with a bucket of orange paint, some brushes and a stepladder. The idea was to paint the easyJet telephone number on the side of the thirteen-metre long scale model of Concorde that used to be parked outside the road tunnels at the main entrance to Heathrow airport. I often wonder what might have happened if we'd actually gone for it. Would we have made the front pages with the audacity of our stunt or would we have perished, Bonnie-and-Clyde style, in a hail of bullets at the hands of the airport police?

But it wasn't just the marketing of easyJet that attracted Stelios' attention: he seemed to have an interest in almost every part and process within his airline. His grasp of business and finance was exceptional, he clearly "got" technology and there was no one better at negotiating with suppliers. He had a quick intellect, a remarkable ability to simplify problems and a good nose for bullshit. On the debit side, there was no doubt that Stelios was hugely opinionated and, at times, as stubborn as a mule (although he could be moved). If you were trying to convince him about something, the best approach was to stand your ground. He'd look hard for weaknesses in your argument, but if you didn't back down and had a strong case he was prepared to change his mind. The good news was that if you convinced Stelios, then that was invariably enough for things to start to happen. Decisions could be taken at the speed a start-up needs, to avoid missing opportunities and losing momentum. For those of us accustomed to presenting business cases to endless committees and board meetings, this kind of accelerated decision-making was a refreshing experience.

In my view, if Stelios had a weakness it was on the people side. On the surface, he was friendly enough with a good sense of humour and a certain amount of natural charm. But underneath, I felt, he found it difficult to really trust anyone. He showed little interest in what was going on outside of work in the lives of his management team. It was also disappointing that at times Stelios seemed to want to take personal credit for everything. The achievements of other individuals in the easyJet success story were rarely acknowledged publicly. Once asked in an interview to describe Stelios in a single word, I came up with "unique" had they asked for three words instead, I would have appended "...thank God".

It wouldn't be fair, however, to end this chapter on a negative note. Simply put, without Stelios there would have been no easyJet. None of the start-up team would have experienced the adrenaline rush and sense of pride that comes from being a part of a successful new business, let alone a piece of aviation history. As a boss, he was simultaneously dynamic, inspiring, challenging and infuriating. But, at the end of the day, the big decisions always came down to him - and most of the time he called them right.

Gorilla bashing

"You've got two chances: Slim and none and Slim's just left town," (Boxing promoter, Don King)

It isn't hard to cast a company like British Airways in the role of an 800-pound Gorilla and an appropriate Goliath with whom easyJet's David could do battle.

But we were to find that the biggest challenge in starting a fight with the BA Gorilla was waking him up in the first place. In the autumn of 1995, as easyJet's two leased planes shuttled up and down between Scotland and Luton, BA steadfastly refused to publicly acknowledge our existence. For the first couple of weeks, our provocative advertising campaign was met with silence. It was starting to get frustrating. Keeping things low key and out of the headlines is probably the best strategy a Gorilla can adopt and an awkward approach to combat. We badly needed a fight if we were to generate the awareness we needed to keep the phones ringing and our planes full.

Then, suddenly and surprisingly, British Airways succumbed to its basic instincts with a typical Gorilla mistake. Having said that easyJet's fares were unsustainable, BA countered our £29 one-way prices with a £58 return fare of its own, albeit requiring an overnight stay and with limited availability. Glasgow and Edinburgh started to feature regularly in BA's tactical promotion of "World Offers", though the company denied that any of this was designed to dislodge the foothold that the upstart young airline had gained on these routes. At easyLand, Stelios called a council of war at which he decided that the best form of defence was to attack. In mid November 1995, we took the decision to offer all unsold seats at our lowest fare of £29 for travel up to Christmas. This meant forgoing significant amounts of revenue, but it made for a simpler marketing proposition and was impossible for British Airways to match.

For the first time since our launch, I was nervous. For me, this was the moment of truth. If we couldn't fill our planes even when we offered all our seats at £29, how would we ever fill them at the higher prices we needed in order to become profitable? We decided to raise the stakes once more, throwing our marketing plans out of the window. We scrambled to buy almost every advertising slot we could find. Full-page advertisements in the *London Evening Standard* and the Scottish press, wall-to-wall radio advertising and, incredibly, even a TV advertising campaign cobbled together in a matter of days. With advertising slots difficult to obtain at short notice in a tight, pre-Christmas market, we were struggling to spend the money. Mike Hellens, the MD of our media-buying agency, Matters Media, was called into the offices to explain why we were having problems getting the level of coverage we wanted. In no uncertain terms, he was told to find a way of spending a million pounds. Otherwise, he'd be fired. Mike shrugged. He was on commission, but to spend that kind of money we'd need to get on television. Without any hesitation, Stelios approved. This was the kind of big, bold, getting-on-the-front-foot decision he liked.

Conventional wisdom dictates that it takes at least a month to make a television ad. Indeed, many creative agencies will want as much as three months. We managed it in less than a week. The creative execution was awful - so awful, it reminded me of one of the cheap curry-house ads you see if you arrive too early to watch a film at the cinema. Featuring a hand holding a model easyJet plane aloft, it was so bad some people thought we'd deliberately made it that way to underline the fact that we didn't waste customers' money on expensive advertising. Fortunately, the price message trumped the ad quality and had the desired effect of making the phones in the call centre ring off the hooks. If you're selling coloured water with sugar in it, like some nameless soft-drink companies, you need to spend millions on artistic ads to build the brand. On the other hand, if you're selling flights to Scotland for £29 at a time when no one else comes close, then - provided the customers accept your planes won't fall out of the sky - the product should sell itself.

During this phase of the airline's growth, Stelios was like a man possessed. And the atmosphere at easyLand was electric. At one stage, we were working six or seven days a week, our days peppered with crisis meetings and calls to action. I had one eye constantly on what Stelios had nicknamed "the till", a computer screen that gave a constantly updating picture of what we'd sold so far that day. When the boss was out of the office, every phone call he made to me was prefaced with the words "what's the till?" And if he didn't like the number I gave him, this was swiftly followed up with "...and what are you doing about it?" In the face of any kind of emerging threat, Stelios rarely waited to see what would happen, he hated inaction.

Generally speaking, starting a business does not go hand in hand with healthy living. As the stress of long working days and poor eating habits began to take their toll, easyJet's management team and its Chairman started to pile on the pounds. It's just as well that a balanced diet is not a pre-requisite for taking on a corporate Gorilla. In the airline's start-up phase, the only things growing faster than easyJet's sales were the ballooning waistlines of a management team subsisting on cold pizza, Kentucky Fried Chicken and bucket-sized cups of Coca Cola. The only exercise many of us were getting was the walk between our office and the airport terminal building to restock our food supplies. We joked that if British Airways didn't get us, a heart attack would!

Nevertheless, our strategy of holding fast and blanketing the country with advertising worked. Sales responded and BA got the message: Stelios had deep pockets and he wasn't going to be bullied out of the market. There was to be no quick knock-out, we'd taken the Gorilla's best shots and were still standing. The bell sounded for the end of the first round. British Airways throttled back on its discounted promotion of the Scottish routes, and I breathed a sigh of relief. Defying the predictions of many within the industry, easyJet had made it to Christmas and, true to form, we celebrated with a big party.

While fighting hard to fill our flights to Glasgow and Edinburgh, we were also preparing the launch of easyJet services between Luton and Aberdeen. The route between London and Scotland's oil capital was a phenomenal money spinner for the UK flag carrier. It held the distinction of having the highest proportion of British Airways Gold Card holders anywhere on its global network. A few years earlier, BA had successfully seen off a challenge from a little known start-up airline called Aberdeen London Express, nicknamed Alex by its passengers and staff. Having dealt with Alex, BA was – I suspect - anticipating that it would have little difficulty seeing off this latest upstart trying to encroach on the pot of gold that the Aberdeen route represented.

Making an impact in Aberdeen itself was crucial in easyJet's efforts to establish its brand and build awareness. But not only did BA seem to have a stranglehold on advertising opportunities across the city, the dominant local newspaper was also highly expensive for a regional title. I was worried: we were running out of time and the load factor (percentage of seats filled) wasn't where we needed it to be. After careful planning and subterfuge, we managed to secure a number of key advertising sites within the airport terminal building. These sites were strategically positioned around the BA check-in desks and above the luggage carousels where the frequent flyers we'd nicknamed the "Fat Cats" collected their bags. Our booking of the poster sites was viewed with some trepidation by those responsible for granting advertising copy clearance at the airport, so much so that I received a phone call warning me that our poster designs would be subject to close scrutiny prior to approval. It was made crystal clear that even the mildest attack on British Airways would not be tolerated. Sensing an opportunity, we drew up the most outrageous copy we could think of - including a design with the tagline "Beware! Thieves operate in this airport" written in BA's corporate colours and submitted for the site above the BA check-in desk. The anticipated rejection duly arrived in the shape of a terse fax, triggering a strategic leak to the media and sensationalist headlines in the local press. "New airline's adverts banned" was the front-page headline in the *Aberdeen Press and Journal*. As we celebrated the black eye we'd just given the 800-pound Gorilla, reports came through that advance sales on the route had started to rise. Some weeks later, on a bitterly cold morning in late January 1996, our first flight from Luton touched down at Aberdeen airport. Once again, it was full.

Despite this early success, it proved hard work establishing ourselves on the London-to-Aberdeen route. After the initial PR fuelled rush, sales and load factors began to dip. I'd been told that there was always a price at which you could fill any plane on any route. That may have been true, but in the case of Aberdeen in February it appeared the price you'd need to charge would be negative - and we weren't ready to start paying people to fly! The problem was the business travellers. Based on "counting the suits", we knew we had some, but not nearly enough. From an early stage, easyJet's natural constituency of small and medium-sized companies had come across in large numbers. Often, these were the guys paying out of their own pockets or working for companies operating with tight margins. The long-term viability of the route hinged on our ability to make inroads into the big oil companies that accounted for the bulk of regular traffic on the route. The oil giants booked mainly through large business travel agents. Back then most of these big agencies wouldn't touch easyJet with a bargepole. The real problem, however, was the fact that a significant proportion of the travellers between London and Aberdeen were wedded to their frequent-flyer programmes.

In an attempt to get back on the front foot, we prepared another salvo for British Airways with the launch of a strident advertising campaign attacking airline loyalty schemes in general and BA's in-house airmiles programme in particular. Stelios had taken the position that frequent.-flyer miles were tantamount to bribery as they tended to be available only on the most expensive fares and, therefore, incentivised corporate travellers to spend more of their company's money. His strength of feeling on this issue was evidenced by the fact that it was soon expressly prohibited to collect airmiles on company business, a condition written into the contracts of easyJet and easyGroup employees.

In need of another attention-grabbing stunt to build momentum behind our anti-airmiles campaign, we came up with the following novel idea: for passengers travelling on this route only, we would offer our own "bribe". Anyone who booked the most expensive easyJet fare of £69 one way would receive a free bottle of whisky. Our low-cost consciousness got the better of us, however, as it was actually a half bottle of cheap whisky which didn't go down too well with some of the passengers queuing up at the Aberdeen sales desk to collect their bribe.

Airmiles itself remained fairly muted throughout this spat, though a subsequent advert published in

The Glasgow Herald did incur its wrath. For the first time, we crossed swords with another fast-growing upstart airline in the shape of Ryanair who had begun operating to Prestwick in Ayrshire, promoting it as "Glasgow Prestwick". Some commentators argued we were a little hypocritical to complain since Prestwick isn't that much further from Glasgow than Luton is from the centre of London, but that didn't stop us. The offending advert was entitled "Ayr Miles" with the sub copy "easyJet fly from Glasgow International not Prestwick". The anticipated reaction came not from Ryanair, who wisely stayed silent, but from Airmiles itself in the form of a solicitor's letter telling us that our use of the expression "Ayr Miles" was a phonetic infringement of its copyright. Stelios' predictable reaction upon seeing this legal warning was to tell me to run the advertisement again.

It would have been quite something if easyJet had succeeded in its mission to eliminate frequent-flier programmes or, at the very least, to bring wholesale changes to the way in which they operate. Perhaps we should not be too surprised that the majority of air travellers seem to draw a distinction between how they spend their own money and that of their companies. Today, frequent-flier programmes remain a key weapon in the armoury of the legacy airline Gorillas as they defend their still significant share of the

European business-travel market against the low-cost horde.

With easyJet now flying to Scotland's three largest cities, opportunities for new destinations north of the border were limited. The only other Scottish airport capable of handling large passenger jets was Inverness. During my time as a graduate trainee at British Airways, I'd been asked to write a report on the airline's importance to remote communities, having spent a week flying round the Highlands and Islands. I'd fallen in love with the spectacular scenery and was convinced that the market had significant growth potential. In late spring 1996, I drove from Aberdeen to Inverness to meet with the airport's commercial director. We'd already established that there were no significant discounts on offer, but I was hoping we might get some marketing support to help us promote the route. The reception I received was decidedly unenthusiastic. My suspicion was that the airport's management was far more interested in airlines offering direct flights from continental Europe than a new budget airline potentially undermining BA's significant traffic to the Highlands. From a financial standpoint, this would be a far from clear-cut decision for easyJet. Inverness was twenty minutes' flying time further north than Glasgow or Edinburgh and, consequently, more expensive. Despite some misgivings, I lobbied hard within easyJet for us to operate the route and was delighted when we got the go-ahead.

Inverness itself had a relatively small population. With just one flight a day timed in the early afternoon, there was no prospect of capturing passengers travelling down to London for a day's business. We would be dependent on highly seasonal tourist traffic to fill our aircraft. This route would provide a real test of our ability to compete. We racked our brains in the search for cost-effective opportunities to bait the British Airways Gorilla. One particular stunt involved Stelios scuba diving in Loch Ness looking for the BA low fare ("everyone's heard of it, but no one's ever found it") but this was aborted due to inclement weather. We were starting to learn that you didn't always have to go through with a stunt in order to get publicity out of the original idea.

We worked closely with the Scottish Tourist Board to promote the appeal of the Highlands to Londoners, jointly funding poster ads on London Underground and even painting a cartoon version of the Loch Ness monster on the side of one of our planes. After a slow start (believe me, the Highlands are a tough sell in winter!), Inverness turned a corner: load factors were lower compared with the other Scottish destinations, but the revenues were higher than anticipated. Importantly, we'd proved that the easyJet formula could work for a leisure-dominated route. With four Scottish destinations under our belt in our first twelve months of operation, we published an orange credit-card-sized airline timetable, recouping the printing costs by selling advertising on the back. It was a small token of our success, but somehow it felt like we'd passed another milestone.

The Gorilla strikes back

"In the fight between you and the world, back the world." (Kafka)

It's an unwritten rule of Gorilla Marketing that the time to be most on your guard is when things appear to be going well. Never underestimate your simian opponent, particularly when he appears to be on the back foot. Corporate history is littered with the carcasses of upstart companies who successfully launched, but were ruthlessly squashed once they started to threaten lumbering incumbents. What Gorillas lack in the speed department they tend to make up for with their two primary weapons; brute force and guile. It had become clear that easyJet wasn't going to be pummelled into submission, but we needed to be on our toes, the Gorilla was about to change tack.

In November 1996, with easyJet established on the Anglo-Scottish routes and flushed with success from its first raids into Europe, British Airways made an unexpected approach. Chief Executive, Bob Ayling, invited Stelios around for tea and a chat at the company's west-London offices, telling him: "I think you've cracked it". To our surprise, it seemed that BA was contemplating buying a stake in easyJet. Discussions continued through the winter of 1996 before BA, somewhat feebly, informed us that the negotiations were to be broken off. They had apparently formed a view that the deal was unlikely to secure regulatory approval. Stelios' fury at this rebuttal was accentuated when, in October 1997, British Airways announced its intention to launch its own low-cost airline. Initially it was called "Go fly", before being shortened to "Go". Within hours of learning of BA's decision, Stelios was on the phone to the lawyers reportedly arguing

"There's no point in waiting until you're out of business. Sue and sue early". Our founder believed BA had tricked him by expressing interest in investing in his airline with the sole objective of getting close to our secrets. The acquired knowledge had then been applied in the creation of Go which he described as a photocopy of the easyJet business plan. Needless to say, British Airways denied any duplicity, but it was a key turning point - both for easyJet and its Chairman. From that point on, Stelios redoubled his efforts, focussing all his energy on winning a war which, it seemed, had now become personal.

Our public stance was that BA was incapable of running a low-cost airline. Indeed, history suggests that budget airlines started by conventional carriers are even more prone to failure than independently-funded start-ups. However, for all our outward bravado, I personally believed that Go would prove to be a more serious competitor than some of my colleagues imagined. I remembered Barbara Cassani, Go's Chief Executive, from my days as a graduate trainee with British Airways back in 1990: bright, articulate and sassy, she stood out in a sea of grey suits. Cassani was seen as a real high flier with potential for the very top, and this was to be her chance for glory. What's more, she had assembled a good team of people around her, including operations supremo, Jane Willacy, an immensely capable individual with whom I'd worked closely at BA and admired greatly.

Initially, the plan had been to concentrate our marketing fire on BA, the 800-pound Gorilla that Stelios believed was pulling the strings, rather than "Go" itself. This was a deliberate move: we wanted to avoid creating awareness for our new competitor, and it also made for better PR. "David versus the slightly bigger boy from the next village" will never make the news, but "David versus Goliath" is always going to make for a good story. We were determined this would be a war waged in full public view. In late 1997, full-page advertisements were placed in a number of the national newspapers, using the analogy of *Beauty and the Beast*. BA Chief Executive, Robert Ayling, and Barbara Cassani were respectively depicted in the two roles. The ads were intended to question the motives of British Airways in starting a low-cost airline. We contended that its motive in setting up Go was to put easyJet out of business before raising its fares again. Like most of our tactical campaigns, it was put together at lightning speed - and was a lot of fun. We found an attractive picture of the Go Chief Executive and searched hard for the most unflattering picture of Ayling we could find. The campaign wasn't cheap: some of the newspaper ads cost upwards of £10,000, but the stakes were high.

Aside from the press, our other key battleground was to be the courts. Stelios wanted the best legal brains on the case. Our QC was to be Robert Webb who, ironically, was to become BA's chief in-house lawyer some years later. Sitting with Stelios in Robert Webb's chambers at an early briefing, I smiled at the legal eagle's business card featuring a cartoon alligator and the inscription "Settle? Where's the fun in that?" I suspected this was one action that wouldn't be settled easily, but we might well have some fun along the way.

Immediately seizing the initiative, Stelios applied for an injunction to stop the gestating airline in its tracks. It was always going to be a long shot that our legal efforts to prevent Go from taking off would be successful, but we reckoned that a high-profile battle would keep us in the headlines - and BA on the back foot. It had the added benefit of distracting Go's senior management and diverting resources away from the herculean task of starting a new airline. At the very least they would have a few sleepless nights worrying about how to deal with tens of thousands of pre-booked passengers if easyJet were to win the case.

On 13th May 1998, with the new airline in the final stages of preparation ahead of its launch, Judge Tuckey delivered his High Court verdict. The application by easyJet for an injunction to stop Go from taking off was struck out. There were some crumbs of comfort in the wording of the judgement, and I recall we proclaimed some kind of victory, but with hindsight it didn't really matter. What counted was that the phoney war with what Stelios was now describing as "BA's low-cost clone" had entered a new phase.

The list of easyJet publicity stunts is certainly long. Arguably, however, the most effective and memorable came with the inaugural flight of Go. On the morning that the fledgling airline's tickets went on sale, I called its booking line and bought ten seats on the first flight from Stansted to Rome. At the time, we didn't exactly know what we were going to do, but by booking the seats we gave ourselves two months to plan our tactics. We'd hoped to have the advantage of surprise but Go didn't have an internet-booking facility at the time. What's more, the name "Stelios Haji-Ioannou" was instantly recognised by the reservations agent who took my call. Sure enough, when our booking confirmation letters arrived, a polite, personal note had been scribbled on them by Barbara Cassani, Go's Chief Executive, wishing us a pleasant flight. On the day itself, we arrived early, assembling in the Stansted Hilton to put on bright orange boiler suits and baseball caps. The outfits were emblazoned on the front with the easyJet logo, with a large letter printed in white on the back. When we stood in line, the letters spelled "Go, easyJet". It was a beautiful sunny morning and the easyJet team was in high spirits as we posed for photographs outside the hotel.

In good time for check-in, we showed up at the airport in our colourful garb. The look on the faces of Go's PR team had to be seen to be believed. Someone called the airport police, but they just laughed and said we were doing nothing wrong. Under the circumstances, Barbara Cassani herself took the upstaging with good grace, even presenting easyJet's Chairman with his own outsized boarding pass. I must confess to having felt some guilt at having hi-jacked Go's big day. If Stelios was feeling any guilt, he certainly wasn't showing it. I can still recall the huge smile on his face as he walked up and down the aisle of the Rome-bound plane, dispensing free easyJet flight vouchers to eager Go passengers. The journalists whom Go had invited to travel with it on its inaugural flight flocked to the back of the plane to interview the owner of its biggest rival. It was quite a coup.

I travelled back from Rome on a flight operated by yet another low-cost operator, the bizarrely named Debonair. Under the leadership of veteran airline executive, Franco Mancassola, Debonair had opted for the middle ground between low-cost and full-service airlines that was to prove disastrous for a number of other start-up airlines, including KLM's Buzz. Its marketing proposition was described to me as "low-cost with a few frills", a concept I likened to being "half-pregnant" and equally unviable. An early and, as it turned out, rather prescient poster advertisement showed Debonair's Finance Director at Franco's feet in tears at the low fares it was offering. As Debonair came under financial pressure in 1998, it put out feelers to easyJet. I went with Stelios to visit Franco in his Luton offices. Franco was charming, cracked jokes and served great coffee - but it was clear that Debonair had nothing to offer us. As we walked out through their car park, Stelios joked to me that Debonair's only asset of any value was Franco's Alfa Romeo. The following year, Debonair went into administration. Naturally enough, we blamed British Airways. Stelios said BA had "blood on its hands".

As predicted, Go had chosen to base itself at Stansted, its first three routes (Milan, Rome and Copenhagen) avoiding any head-to-head competition with easyJet. However, in the second half of 1998, Go announced a new service flying three times daily to Edinburgh at similar fares to those offered by easyJet. Stelios was not happy, to put it mildly - particularly when Go then lowered its fares still further, undercutting our prices. With the original legal action in the UK courts still in the background, an additional complaint was lodged with the European Competition Authorities alleging predatory pricing and cross-subsidisation.

A ding-dong advertising and PR battle between the two carriers soon developed. Go was now fighting back, giving easyJet a taste of its own medicine. When a dusting of snow closed Luton airport, Go took out ads saying "Would you rather fly with the airline most likely to get you there or the airline with a generous refund policy because they don't?" David Magliano, Go's Sales & Marketing Director, celebrated its triumph in the "best low-cost carrier" airline category at a prestigious awards ceremony by taking a long-term poster site close to easyJet's headquarters.

Weathering the storm of provocative advertising and constant sniping in the media from its orange rival, Go continued to expand. It opened a new hub in Bristol and scaled up its Stansted operation, offering new services to a host of summer-sun destinations. The battle moved closer to easyLand when Go poached a number of key staff, including operations guru, Andy Holmes, and Mike Coltman, easyJet's contracts manager. I viewed this as a smart move on Go's part: I'd got to know Mike when we both went out to visit Southwest Airlines in New Orleans. He was a clever guy, personable and charismatic with a wicked sense of humour. More than anyone, Mike understood the importance of company culture and the role it had played in the Southwest success story.

In late 1998, I took a big decision of my own. Stelios told me of his plans to set up a string of new ventures under the "easy" brand. I would be the Marketing Director of the "easyGroup", working with him to develop and launch these new ideas. The first of these would be a string of giant internet cafés throughout Europe and, eventually, the world (well, it seemed a good idea at the time!). I would be made a Director of both easyGroup and the new start-ups as well as being given a chance to invest alongside him. Leaving easyJet would mean stepping away from the battle with British Airways just when it was getting interesting. Yet it was clear that, although the airline was continuing to grow fast, it was maturing and entering a new phase. I'd also started to develop differences of opinion with Ray Webster, the Managing Director whom Stelios had brought in from Air New Zealand two years previously. Ray, a trained engineer with many years of airline experience, had an analytical approach that contrasted markedly with my reliance on intuition. He was to play a key role in guiding easyJet through its successful flotation two years later and can take significant credit for the airline's success. Stelios counselled me that I was better at starting things up and growing them in the early stages and that now was the time to move on. It was hard advice to swallow, but with the benefit of hindsight, I guess he was right. At an emotional leaving party to celebrate the move to easyGroup, I was presented with the bright orange boiler suit I'd worn on our famous Go raid a few months earlier.

While I was dealing with the challenges of starting new easy-branded businesses in the white heat of the internet boom years, Go continued to build its network, inching towards profitability. With its budget offspring now firmly established, tensions began to develop within British Airways over the future of a potential problem child. Go's success had started to raise questions about competition with its larger parent on European routes. By now, Bob Ayling - who'd got BA into the low-cost game in the first place - was on his way out. His replacement as Chief Executive was to be Australian, Rod Eddington, a man on a mission to strengthen the flag carrier's financial position. Speculation intensified that the low-cost airline was in play.

The issue looked to have been settled early in 2001 when, following an auction, BA announced that it was to sell Go to a management-buyout team working in partnership with private-equity group, 3i. Most commentators assumed that the new owners would recoup their investment by floating the airline at some point down the line. But the real bombshell was yet to come.

One day in March 2002, by now no longer working for Stelios, I was in my car en route to Peterborough when I switched on the radio to listen to the news. What I heard nearly caused me to swerve off the road. Apparently, easyJet was to take-over its arch rival, Go, in a transaction valued at £374 million. It was a masterstroke! The deal catapulted easyJet into the Premier League of European airlines and consolidated Stelios' reputation as a dealmaker and a real player in global aviation. After years of fighting toe to toe with British Airways, he'd landed a knockout punch. The 800-pound Gorilla had hit the canvas and his victory over them was complete.

Going international

"European customers will crawl bollock-naked over broken glass to get low fares." (Michael O'Leary)

Although we began life as a domestic operator, shuttling up and down to Scotland, easyJet was conceived as a pan-European airline. The size of the

European market as a whole was comparable with the size of the North American market where the low-cost model had demonstrated its long-term viability. Although, on paper, the scale of opportunity between the two markets was similar, an airline expanding into Europe faced a number of additional challenges. These included the obvious ones like language and culture, not to mention other differences such as low levels of credit-card ownership and strong vested interests at national level. We couldn't afford to spend millions adapting our model to meet the needs of individual markets. In any case, complexity carries with it significant long-term costs. If easyJet was to work as a truly European airline, it would need as standardised and simple an approach as possible. In the words of Stelios, we needed a "cookie cutter".

A key advantage of the "David versus Goliath" formula - apart from its inherent simplicity - is that it was applicable to virtually all the markets we were intending to enter. Every European country had an incumbent flag carrier and, to a greater or lesser degree, they had grown fat and lazy over the years under the protective umbrella of a regulated market. Hardly surprising, therefore, that we employed the same formula when we made our first foray into Europe with the launch of our Amsterdam service in April 1996. At that time, Holland was Europe's second most deregulated air-transport market, with Amsterdam one of the UK's leading short-break destinations. It was also the home turf of Dutch national carrier, KLM, an industry heavyweight that I counted firmly in the 800-pound gorilla category. While regarded with a measure of pride by the country's nationals, KLM had prospered on the back of its domination of its small domestic market and a pre-eminent position at Schipol airport, a key international hub.

With a growing base of satisfied customers and strong awareness in Luton and the surrounding counties, we were confident about generating sales at the UK end of the route. We launched our service with a headline-grabbing offer. Amsterdam priced at 39p for all seats on the first day, exclusively promoted through the *Daily Mirror*. But, for the route to be profitable, we'd also need to generate sales from the Dutch market where our name was virtually unknown. In the weeks leading up to the first flight, we plastered bright orange posters across central Amsterdam and placed display advertisements highlighting KLM's high fares in the major Dutch newspapers. This time round, we managed to secure the key poster sites we wanted, having engaged the services of Jaap Boender who knew the Dutch media market inside out. Just as BA had done before it, KLM ignored our provocation and maintained a stony silence. It was time to poke them with a sharp stick.

Gorilla-baiting was starting to be fun, and Stelios came up with a good idea: in advance of our launch, we'd printed coupons in our in-flight magazine, inviting passengers to complain about the ridiculously high price of flights to Amsterdam. Appropriately incentivised, this had solicited a massive response which we bagged up in four large sacks before setting off to hand deliver them to the President of KLM, a Mr Pieter Bouw at the airline's Amsterdam offices with camera crews following our every move. Needless to say, we were turned away at the security gatehouse (although a KLM representative did at least have the good grace to come down and collect them). A specially staged press conference at Schipol was well attended by the media (though ignored by KLM). What's more, easyJet made prime-time news on all the major Dutch TV channels. Provoked by the positive coverage we were receiving, the Dutch Gorilla could contain itself no longer. KLM released a press statement predictably rubbishing the no-frills concept and explaining why it wasn't going to work in the Dutch market. Within minutes of our press conference going on air, the calls from Amsterdam started coming through. The Dutch, it seemed, liked low fares after all.

For all their public denials, KLM were undoubtedly worried by the arrival of easyJet on their doorstep. Within a matter of weeks they introducing fare cuts on flights between London and Amsterdam, prompting an allegation that they were engaged in predatory pricing. Not for the last time easyJet went to the European Commission, bolstered by the uncovering of an internal KLM memo which allegedly called for "a determined campaign to stop the growth and development of easyJet". The Competition Commission has sharp teeth with the ability to impose fines of up to ten per cent of turnover for offenders. The action likely caused other flag carriers throughout Europe to sit up and take notice. Though the complaint ended up going nowhere, the ongoing battle was widely discussed in the media. In a few short months and at relatively low cost, easyJet had gone from being an unknown company to a recognised brand in the Dutch market.

Three years later, in belated acknowledgement that the low-cost model had something to offer after all, KLM announced the creation of Buzz, its own low-cost carrier based at Stansted airport. The new airline was doomed from the start: not only was the business model fundamentally flawed, but the airline chose to operate with a mixed fleet, including the British Aerospace 146, an aircraft totally unsuited to a low-cost operation. For a few short years, the purple-and-yellow-liveried airline struggled to establish itself in a low-cost market that was now starting to look crowded. On routes to Austria and France, Buzz soon found itself competing head-to-head with Ryanair and Go, they tried switching to new routes but to no avail. The cost disadvantage they were carrying was simply unsustainable. Buzz had turned up to a gunfight armed with a knife. Realising its mistake, KLM started looking for a way out, exploring options for a sale or merger. The airline's demise finally came when Buzz was taken over, swallowed up and spat out by Ryanair. Few mourned its passing.

To manage easyJet's growth in the Dutch market, we'd taken on Ivar Gribnau, a young, ambitious graduate from the University of Leiden looking to break into the airline business. The job of Marketing Manager for the Netherlands was never advertised. Ivar simply badgered me for days on end with telephone calls from Holland offering his services. In the end, I agreed to an interview just to get the guy off the phone. It proved to be a smart move on my part. Not only was Ivar a great find, we'd also stumbled on a formula that would serve us well. For each market we appointed someone to the role of national marketing manager, giving them responsibility for getting "bums on seats". At the weekly marketing meetings, we would run through route-performance reports, capacity projections, advertising plans and competitor performance. Because our operation was direct sale only, and tickets non-refundable, we had a real-time picture of how each route was performing and could respond quickly to fill seats and maximise revenue. This was in marked contrast to my experiences working at British Airways where the complexity of the airline's pricing and multi-channel distribution made tactical marketing of this kind significantly more challenging.

Throughout 1996 and into 1997, easyJet's expansion into Europe gathered momentum, the versatility of the giant-killer formula being demonstrated to great effect. Although the launch of a new service between Luton and Nice brought us into competition with Air France for the first time, our key opponent was, once again, British Airways. The national carrier dominated the route with high-frequency services from several UK airports. Its prices were high, as you might expect given the well-heeled reputation of those travelling to Nice. We believed BA had been running the route as a cash cow for years. Lower fares would stimulate the market and provide sufficient demand to fill our planes. People with second homes were a key target market, and word of mouth was very strong among this group: we were receiving several calls a week from property owners, pleading for us to start flights to the French Riviera.

We launched with a bang, flying sixty prize winners from three UK regional radio stations down to Nice for a party at local nightspot, Wayne's Bar. Stelios was in celebratory mood: he would no longer have to fly to his home in the south of France on a competitor airline. For the first time, I spotted him on the dance floor, strutting his stuff to the sound of the classic Oasis classic "Don't Look Back in Anger". The prize winners had been accompanied to Nice by presenters from the radio stations involved. The event proved a sound investment - we got great coverage from the launch party, not to mention plenty of on-air messages for our new service. For once, we didn't really need it. We didn't even need to put a provocative poster above the British Airways sales desk at Nice airport, but we did it anyway - and it felt pretty good! Fares were higher than for the domestic routes, with prices between £49 and £99 each way. Even so, seats were selling like hot cakes as word of easyJet's arrival spread like wildfire through second home owners and the expatriate community in the south of France.

By now, we'd established a pattern and moved speedily onto Spain and the Catalan capital, Barcelona. The city was a popular short-break destination with UK travellers, underserved and with plenty of potential to grow. Our Spanish marketing manager, Christina Bernabe, knew exactly what to do. We adopted the same approach that had served us so well for previous routes, achieving a similar result. By this stage, our UK advertising was becoming more cost-effective since we were able to list multiple destinations in our classified press ads. We reprinted our expanding timetable, this time with a picture showing our modest route network on the reverse.

Computer analysis of our passenger's postcodes showed that, with the launch of international services, easyJet's catchment area had widened: we were now attracting customers from across the country. A significant proportion of them were travelling down to Luton from the north of England. In the spring of 1997, negotiations began with the owners of Liverpool airport with a view to making it easyJet's second UK base. Speke airport (since renamed Liverpool John Lennon Airport) had been in the shadow of its larger rival, Manchester, for many years. Like Luton two years earlier, Liverpool airport was underused. Owners, The Peel Group, were ambitious, and there was a deal to be done. On a visit up to Liverpool to assess opportunities for branding our airport presence, I was struck by the similarities with Luton two years earlier. We moved quickly: by the end of the year, easyJet was operating flights to both Amsterdam and Nice from Liverpool.

Opening a second UK base gave easyJet some important strategic leverage with Luton airport, the ownership of which was rumoured to be on the verge of changing hands. With easyJet projecting rapid growth and other low-cost airlines knocking on Luton's door, a new owner might be tempted to impose higher airport charges. In this eventuality, having the option of putting additional capacity into Liverpool rather than Luton would be a useful bargaining chip - and a potential insurance policy, so it proved.

Less than two years had passed since our first flight, but we had proved the airline was financially viable. The time had come for Stelios to spend real money. By the autumn of 1997, he felt sufficiently confident to place an order for twelve new Boeing 737-300 aircraft. The price paid was a carefully guarded secret, but I suspected he'd got a great deal. With the deal agreed, Boeing bosses rashly offered to take the easyJet senior management team to the restaurant of our choice for a celebratory dinner. Stelios had no hesitation in nominating the world famous Hotel de Paris restaurant in Monaco, renowned for its mouth-watering food and eye-watering prices. It would mean putting on a tie for the evening - only the second time I'd had to wear one since joining easyJet - but the meal was worth it, and I like to think we put a small dent in Boeing's annual profits that evening!

Stelios' Greek heritage meant that our launch of services between London and Athens in the summer of 1998 was always going to be a high-profile battle. However, in one respect we were faced with an unprecedented dilemma. Olympic

Airlines, the Greek flag carrier, was in a truly parlous financial state and there was no PR mileage to be had in picking on such an obviously weak competitor. Instead, we turned our attention back to an old enemy in the shape of the Greek travel-agency community, running a series of impolite, mocking ads encouraging the travelling public to cut out the middleman. The agents obtained a court injunction preventing us from running the ads in the Greek press. We responded by painting the offending expression in six-foot high lettering on the side of one of our aeroplanes before flying it down to Athens. The agents rose to the bait in style, launching a high-profile legal action culminating in a court appearance in Athens by Stelios himself. Prior to the court hearing, easyJet's Chairman had announced that he would be offering vouchers for free flights to London to anyone who turned out to support him at the trial. On emerging from the courtroom, Stelios was greeted by a horde of people chanting his name, all anxious to get their hands on the free flight vouchers. Among them, a number of travel agents were spotted. A chaotic scene developed, with the crowd scrambling for the vouchers as easyJet's call-centre manager, John MacLeod, doubling as Stelios' unofficial minder, fought to extract his boss from the melee. Happily, the only lasting injuries were those to the pride of the Greek travel-agency community.

Indeed, the whole incident has become part of easyJet folklore.

In the spring of 1999, easyJet turned its attention to the lucrative Swiss market. Switzerland was not a member of the European Union and was not, therefore, bound by the European Open Skies agreements that had done so much to open up free market competition between airlines accustomed to cosy duopolies. Both conventional and low-cost carriers looked on the Zurich and Geneva routes with envious eyes as the seasonality of skiing traffic ran counter-cyclical to the summer-sun destinations that generated so much of their revenue. The frequency of flights to places like Malaga, Faro and Alicante could be cut back for the winter, with the aircraft redeployed to pick up the skiing market.

But, without the support of the regulators in Brussels, there was only one way to build a sizeable operation between the UK and Switzerland - and that was through the acquisition of an existing Swiss carrier. When Stelios got to hear that a Swiss part-charter, part-scheduled operator called TEA was running into difficulties, he seized his chance and snapped up a share in the carrier for a budget price. The airline's base was moved from Basle to Geneva and easyJet Switzerland was born. With frequent, low-cost flights from London to (first) Geneva and (later) Zurich, easyJet rapidly took market share from British Airways and Swissair who could scarcely believe what was happening to them. However, it was when easyJet announced that it was intending to operate flights out of Switzerland to other European destinations that the gloves really came off. A legal notice from the Swiss authorities on the eve of easyJet's first flight from Geneva to Barcelona in July 1999 forced the airline to refund all monies paid by passengers. Unabashed, Stelios made an announcement on board the inaugural flight explaining our battle against the Swissair monopoly. He then passed a hat (some contend it was actually a bucket) around and collected a significant proportion of the money that had been given back to the passengers. It was a nice touch, but you can't run an airline funded through charitable contributions. What easyJet needed was a way of highlighting the intrinsic unfairness of the protectionist ruling and getting the wider Swiss public on its side. That's where the tents came in.....

Above the easyLand reception there used to hang a small, nondescript two-man tent. Visitors to the airline's headquarters were often puzzled to see it hanging there. Those that asked were surprised to learn that this was an unlikely trophy of a famous victory over Swissair. The Swiss carrier's attempts to block easyJet's operations between Geneva and Barcelona were based on an arcane ruling that its low-cost flights must come with accommodation provided. To adhere to the technical legalities, easyJet erected a small number of orange tents on the side of a hill, one hundred and fifty kilometres north of Barcelona. Only a handful of brave souls ever stayed in them.

The move was widely reported in the Swiss media, not only exposing the device which, easyJet believed, was being employed to keep them out of the market, but also turning the national carrier into a laughing stock. Calls and internet enquiries from Swiss customers rose sharply. Eventually, the authorities - undoubtedly embarrassed - dropped their objections.

Today, former proud national symbol Swissair, the airline that fought unsuccessfully to stem the low-cost tide, is but one more name on a lengthening casualty list in a brutally unforgiving industry. It's incredible to think that a flimsy tent purchased from Argos for £29.99 could have played such a significant part in its downfall. It's just a shame that, in recording for posterity the quasi-Shakespearean tragedy of Swissair's demise, the newspaper editors missed the opportunity to use the headline "Now is the winter of our discount tent".

With easyJet's foothold on the continent firmly established and a number of European aviation's 800-pound Gorillas sporting black eyes and bloody noses, this part of the story draws to a close. The airline's initial forays into Europe had proved a real education and shone a torch into some of the darkest corners of protectionism. What amazed me, perhaps more than anything, was how flag carriers faced with the entry of a low-cost airline into their markets had repeated the same basic mistakes. Gorillas are slow learners!

Looking in the mirror

"The creatures outside looked from pig to man, and from man to pig, and from pig to man again; but already it was impossible to say which was which." (George Orwell, Animal Farm)

In April 2000, after an incredible but exhausting five years working for Stelios as Marketing Director of, first, easyJet and, later, easyGroup, I decided it was time for me to move on to new challenges. As is well known, the airline went from strength to strength and today can itself be described as an 800-pound Gorilla of the aviation business. In size alone, easyJet has serious Gorilla credentials, carrying passengers numbering in the tens of millions on over 500 routes between 118 airports. The airline has become a household name, not just in the UK but in a whole host of countries across Europe. By most measures, it can be counted a financial Gorilla too, as evidenced by a stock-market value of well over a billion pounds and the huge amounts of cash held on its balance sheet.

Stelios has become Sir Stelios, a self-styled "serial entrepreneur" and a philanthropist with his own charitable foundation. So far, none of the businesses he subsequently founded has yet come close to matching the success of his airline. easyLand has finally been outgrown and replaced by a larger, orange headquarters building at Luton; the call centre has long closed. The fleet of Boeings has been largely replaced by Airbus aircraft and the once casual cabin-crew uniforms have become progressively smarter and more corporate.

Alongside the perennial challenge of fierce competition, new threats have emerged to the airline's future. Growing consumer awareness of the environmental impact of aircraft emissions and rising fuel prices are close to the top of the list. These will provide testing challenges for easyJet in the years ahead.

From the customer's perspective, there have been some distinctly unwelcome developments. The days when the price you were quoted was the price you paid are long gone. Today, the final cost is inflated by government taxes, luggage charges and iniquitous credit-card fees. The airline's website resembles a vast online bazaar whose persistent electronic merchants whisper seemingly enticing offers in your ear. In the height of summer, passengers waddle, penguin-like, through the terminals, clad in multiple layers of clothing to avoid excess baggage charges. A significant and growing proportion of the airline's revenue is now derived from ancillary services rather than its core business of flying passengers. Airports have got in on the act, too. Airport car-park charges have always been expensive, but now they border on the extortionate. Rocket scientists no longer work at NASA. Instead, they are all employed to think up ever more creative ways to get airline passengers to part with their money. Luton is leading the way, having recently introduced a £2 fee for baggage trolleys and the so-called "kiss-and-drop" charge for the privilege of dropping off travellers at the airport.

As for the people mentioned in this book who helped get the airline off the ground, virtually everyone I ever worked with at easyJet has since moved on. Some have left the aviation industry behind them, others have taken up senior positions at low-cost carriers around the world. Chief Executives and Board Directors, among them big-hitters from the corporate world, have come and gone. Stelios remains, no longer on the easyJet Board, but still an active investor behind the scenes hatching who-knows-what plans for the future.

Yet, when I walk through Luton or Gatwick airports and see the vast array of aircraft in their bright orange livery, I smile to myself and remember easyJet's humble beginnings and our Gorilla Marketing adventures. Those rollercoaster early years when the foundations of the airline's long-term success were laid down.

If this book achieves just one thing I hope it is to demonstrate how a great team of people with the right motivation, the right leadership, access to the right resources and a little dose of good fortune can accomplish remarkable things.

Gorillas everywhere (easyJet included), be warned!

Tony Anderson August 2010